MW00713192

Essential to completing the Great Commission in our generation

Without question, Dr. Bill Bright has helped to reach more people with the message of Christ than anyone else in our generation. Dr. Bright and Dr. Davis, in their latest book, *Beyond All Limits*, is a must-read for all of God's people. I recommend it most heartily.

LARRY BURKETT
Crown Financial Ministries

Bill Bright and James Davis have given us a penetrating look at what the future church must be to reach the future generation. They have shown us the challenge of the future and we must understand it if we are going to have successful church ministry in the future. But, these brothers have reminded us that if we do not base our ministry on the historical message found in the Word of God, we cannot change people in the future. May this book equip many to build a church to meet people in the future.

DR. ELMER L. TOWNS
Dean, Liberty University
Lynchburg, VA

I believe Bill Bright and James O. Davis have hit the nail on the head with their perspective of the synergistic church. To make the most of the tremendous opportunities that are facing us in the 21st century, every leader should be striving to build a church with no roof and no walls. This book will inspire you to remove any limitations and fulfill the powerful potential of the Church of Jesus Christ.

REV. BRIAN HOUSTON
Senior Pastor, Hillsong Church
Sydney, Australia

My dear friends—Bill Bright and James Davis—have crafted a challenging book, *Beyond All Limits*. It is a call to walk a tightrope between two competing concepts, namely, "Change or die!" and "Get with it!" Their balanced conclusion is a synergistic church for a planet in crisis. I concur with their thesis, providing we can state without compromise that we are "laborers together *with* God" (1 Cor. 3:9, KJV). The tendency on the part of all of us is to swing to one extreme or the other. God's way is always the biblical balance.

STEPHEN F. OLFORD
Founder and Senior Lecturer
The Stephen Olford Center for Biblical Preaching

Dr. Bill Bright's and James Davis's passion for evangelism and revival in America has generated a dynamic book that will unite denominations and churches all across the land in obedience to the great commission.

DR. PAUL CUNNINGHAM
General Superintendent, Church of the Nazarene
Kansas City, MO

Beyond All Limits is a powerful tool for an extraordinary vision destined to equip the greatest army of pastors and leaders in Church history. This will be essential to completing the Great Commission in our generation.

DR. DICK EASTMAN
International President, Every Home for Christ

Beyond All Limits is must reading for any pastor or leader at this time in history. This wonderful book explains that in order to lead people during times of trouble and rapid change, the church has to remove the roof and knock down the walls between it and the society to be reached. As Dr. Bright and Dr. Davis so aptly point out: "The church known more for its steeple than its people is a church known more for its past than its present."

The heart cry of this book for a "synergistic" church is, I believe, the heart cry of God. God is looking for churches that are relevant, dynamic, living bodies of believers. This great book will help many achieve the great goal that Christ lays before them of reaching the lost, enabling them to minister beyond the limitations that come against them.

> Rev. Tommy Barnett
> First Assembly of God
> Phoenix, AZ

Bill Bright's and James Davis' new book, *Beyond All Limits*, is a dramatic call to effective ministry in the twenty-first century. They combine the timeless truths of Scripture, the Great Commission to evangelize the world, and a synergistic approach to ministry that "blows the roof off" all our current limitations for reaching people in our generation. Don't miss this powerful call to ministry.

> Dr. Jerry Falwell
> Chancellor, Liberty University
> Lynchburg, VA

This is a book for our times. The biblical principles communicated so clearly and powerfully will profoundly benefit any pastor.

> Howard Dayton
> CEO, Crown Financial Ministries

Beyond All Limits contains a message from the heart of God that will challenge the hearts of those who dare read it. Every pastor and church leader who desires to evangelize and disciple the world in these last days must read and apply the principles in this book.

> Rev. Max Yeary
> Christian Life Center
> Fort Lauderdale, FL

As the world around us changes in historic proportions, pastors and ministry leaders are continuously faced with new challenges. In their book, *Beyond All Limits: The Synergistic Church for a Planet in Crisis*, Bright and Davis offer practical, clear-cut building blocks that are vital to successfully moving forward and effectively impacting those around us. Providing a full spectrum of solid biblical perspectives and fresh timely insights, this comprehensive book is a must-read. Drawing on their years of experience and study, the authors have given us an invaluable tool rich with wisdom, creativity, and strategies that will propel us beyond all limits.

DUTCH SHEETS
Dutch Sheets Ministries

Too easily in this hostile world the Church spends her energy holding the fort when we should be storming the heights for God. Bill Bright and James Davis understand the problem and point the way to revitalization through new strategies and Spirit-filled leadership. Warmly written, the book cannot help but challenge faith and inspire hope.

DR. ROBERT E. COLEMAN
Gordon-Conwell University
Boston, MA

Beyond All Limits: The Synergistic Church for a Planet in Crisis is a volume that reflects a clear connection to the realities of the 21st century. Yet more than merely defining those realities statistically, the authors provide an understandable response to the complexities of 21st century challenges. For serious pastoral leaders, the synergistic church paradigm offers biblical substance and cultural applicability. This model is usable wherever committed church leaders are giving themselves to the task of reaching our world with the gospel.

DR. BYRON D. KLAUS
President, Assemblies of God Theological Seminary
Springfield, MO

Blowing off the roof and knocking down the walls hardly seems like a strategy for renewal. Yet Bright and Davis not only make it seem attractive, but entirely possible. Now, as perhaps never before, we see, really see, that we need each other. Synergism is the key these two mature churchmen use to unlock the door on a 21st-century church, neither staggering nor swaggering, but marching together toward a common goal.

DR. MARK RUTLAND
President, Southeastern College
Lakeland, FL

Experience is a valued commodity received without monetary price tag. Experience that takes one "beyond all limits" is a unique experience, and Dr. Bright and Dr. Davis have generously shared their valuable insights. From the legacy of faithful service, you may expect that our Lord will use the authors to communicate His passion for a needy world.

DR. JOHN CORTS
President, Billy Graham Evangelistic Association

Beyond all Limits: The Synergistic Church for a Planet in Crisis is well overdue. To meet the demands of training national pastors and Christian workers, a new paradigm must be created.

Bill Bright and James Davis have creatively designed a program that challenges traditional thinking and expedites the training of national pastors and ministry leaders.

As one who has lived overseas and ministered in over sixty countries, I immediately recognized that *Beyond All Limits* is deigned to meet a critical need for national church leaders.

DR. DICK WYNN
Vice President, EQUIP

As the technological tidal waves pound the seashores of time, the Church will either ride the waves of innovation or miss the greatest opportunities to impact our world. Dr. Bright and Dr.

Davis reveal to us eight powerful synergistic principles, designed to develop dynamic church leaders. I highly recommend this book to pastors who truly want to be on the cutting-edge of evangelism.

Dr. Robert Schuller
Crystal Cathedral
Garden Grove, CA

I believe that *Beyond All Limits* will be a significant resource for the fulfilling of God's mission in this world—which I believe to be the drawing together of a rescued people in Christ from every time tribe, language, and nation to bring glory to our Father's name. This book provides a challenge to local churches to get close enough to those hellish gates so that they can be pushed back. It also provides fresh and practical help for how the church can be more effective in its Christ-mandated task. May God's Spirit use it to rekindle the passion among our churches that they may go beyond their roofs and walls and carry the good new of Jesus to all people.

Greg Waybright, Ph.D.
President, Trinity Evangelical Divinity School
Deerfield, IL

Dr. Bright and Dr. Davis have provided a landmark book that will impact evangelism around the world. Not only is it theologically sound and intellectually stimulating, but it moves leaders beyond the natural limitation into the Spirit-filled life. I challenge every pastors to read and apply the eight core values to their life and ministry.

Dr. Richard Mouw
Fuller Theological Seminary
Pasadena, CA

Beyond All Limits

The Synergistic Church for a
lanet in Crisis

REWORD BY JOHN C. MAXWELL

NewLife
PUBLICATIONS

ILL BRIGHT·JAMES O. DAVIS

Beyond All Limits: The Synergistic Church for a Planet in Crisis

Published by
NewLife **Publications**
A ministry of Campus Crusade for Christ
P.O. Box 620877
Orlando, FL 32862-0877

Design and production by Genesis Group

Printed in the United States of America

ISBN 1-56399-189-6 (h.c.)

ISBN 1-56399-190-X (p.b.)

Unless otherwise indicated, Scripture quotations are from the *New American Standard Bible*, © 1960, 1962, 1963, 1968, 1971, 1972, 1973, 1975, 1977 by the Lockman Foundation, La Habra, California.

Scripture quotations designated NIV are from the *New International Version*, © 1973, 1978, 1984 by the International Bible Society. Published by Zondervan Bible Publishers, Grand Rapids, Michigan.

Scripture quotations designated TLB are from *The Living Bible*, © 1971 by Tyndale House Publishers, Wheaton, Illinois.

Scripture quotations designated KJV are from the *King James Version,* Public Domain.

*To all pastors worldwide,
who have surrendered their will, suffered in their
walk, served their world, and spoken God's Word
in the power of the Holy Spirit for the single purpose of fulfilling the Great Commission in their
context, community, country, and culture.*

Contents

Foreword

A changing world demands a changing church. Yet, at its very core, the church is unchangeable. This paradox has been the source of debate, struggle, and fear for centuries. How do we share an uncompromised gospel with a world that is changing rapidly around us? What can serve as an anchor to keep us grounded, but also serve as a compass to keep us going in the right direction? Is it possible for the church to significantly influence the culture around it and still maintain the centrality of its message? Can the church move beyond all the limitations that seem to surround it and touch a planet in crisis?

The answer is unequivocally *yes!* We can minister beyond these limits and any others that come against us. But it will take key leaders who are inspired by the Holy Spirit to guide Christians through these new dynamic lands.

The church will rise and fall on its leadership. Therefore, it is necessary to have leaders who are equipped with the right tools to lead the church. And two dynamic leaders who are qualified to help the church maneuver through these changing times are Bill Bright and James O. Davis.

In the last 2,000 years, no individual in the history of the church has been as instrumental in the spreading of the gospel as Bill Bright. I have incredible respect for Bill because he has modeled the way for me and for thousands of other ministry leaders. Next to my father, Bill has had the most influence on my spiritual life. Through the *JESUS* film and the *Four Spiritual Laws*, over 6 billion people have been exposed to the gospel of Jesus Christ. The ministry of Campus Crusade for Christ, which he has lead for fifty years, has touched almost every country of the world and trained hundreds of thousands of workers. Bill Bright's legacy of evangelism and discipleship is phenomenal.

Thousands carry his visions, and millions have come to Christ as a result of his faithfulness. And even now as he nears the end of his life and ministry, he has chosen to partner with James Davis, an international evangelist of over twenty years to more than 60 countries, to launch a global vision to touch, teach, and train more than one million ministers worldwide.

Beyond All Limits is a guidepost for ministry for the future. It represents a fresh wind blowing through the sails of the church. In this book, James and Bill provide you with the maps required to navigate an uncharted, technological landscape. They provide keen insight into the necessary characteristics of the church that will be effective in these new seas of ministry. The church they paint, a church beyond all limits, is one that lives and works in harmony with its Creator and its world. The eight characteristics they've identified are vital to the health and growth of the church. If they are not found in your ministry or church, you will not experience the development God desires of you. And it is through these eight characteristics that the church can maintain the appropriate balance between an unchanging core and a changing culture.

With more people coming to Christ in these trying times than ever before, the principles of synergy and unity in Christ are necessary components to the church of the twenty-first century. It is essential that the Body of Christ join together. We must be a church that worships God in all that we do. We must connect with God so that our lives are lived like Christ wants us to live. We must connect with the lost through compassion and evangelism as Christ has commanded. We must be a church that witnesses to the world. Finally, we must connect with each other in the church through trust and love. As Bill Bright has taught and modeled for years, we must be a church that works together for the cause of Jesus Christ.

DR. JOHN C. MAXWELL
Founder, The INJOY Group

Preface

Every Campus Crusade for Christ worker must be an active member of a local church within ninety days of being assigned to his or her ministry. Why? It is our fundamental belief that God established the Church for the purpose of completing the Great Commission. We believe in the local church. We believe in the local church because it is Jesus Christ's Church. During our combined 80 years of ministry, we have been privileged to travel millions of miles and partner with thousands of churches of all denominations, sizes, styles, and contexts. Each of these wonderful churches contributes in its own unique way to God's mission. Their differences complement each other, creating a beautiful tapestry of different colors and distinctions. When viewed together, they show God's purpose and plan for the Church. We at Campus Crusade for Christ and Cutting Edge International have always seen ourselves as organizations that serve the Church in accomplishing its mission. We have identified eight distinctives that are crucial for dynamic pastoral ministry in today's turbulent environment. It is our hope that these distinctives will help you and your ministry move "beyond your natural limits" into a realm of supernatural impact through the empowerment of the Holy Spirit.

Acknowledgments

This book is the product of synergy among family members, dynamic leaders, and fellow laborers of Christ. A special heartfelt thanks is in order for Randy Jumper, who served tirelessly with us for many months through careful research, writing, and editing; to Helmut Teichert, who provided creative insights and project coordination; to Sheri Davis and Jackie Chrisner, who invested many long hours in editing; to John Barber, who helped with the theological review and final polish of the manuscript; and to Lynn Copeland of Genesis Group, who did the final editing under serious time constraints. Our gratitude goes to Roland Taylor for cover art direction, and Tom Gilleon for the cover and synergistic church illustration. We also want to thank John Nill, publisher, and Michelle Treiber, production coordinator.

Truly, we can do more together than we can by ourselves.

CHAPTER 1

A World in Hyperchange

We live in a world that is rapidly changing. The explosion of technology and information has created an environment of change and innovation that is unprecedented. According to sociologists, the culture shifts that used to take decades are now occurring every few months. This whirlwind of change is overwhelming. It is impossible for anyone to keep pace with all the developments that are taking place in the world.

Through technology, we are becoming a faster-paced and more connected culture than ever before. With the advent of the World Wide Web, global communications are unparalleled. It is now possible to send an "Instant Message" to people on the other side of the world, exchanging information in a matter of seconds. New ways of gathering and utilizing information have revolutionized the institutions of society. And the distribution of knowledge and information is now as important as the creation of new knowledge and the discovery of new information.

In 1969, there were only four primitive websites on the World Wide Web. By 1990, over 333,000 existed. By the end of 1997, there were over 20 million. In 2001, the popular search engine Google.com claims it catalogs over 1.6 billion websites and adds more each day.[1] And according to researcher George Barna, almost 50 million people in the United States alone may soon use the Internet for religious experiences.[2]

The advancements in computing speed and processor power continue to create other dramatic changes in technology. Society is greatly impacted by Moore's Law, which states that the power of computer processing doubles every 18 to 24 months. As a result, the world is moving faster and faster; it is involved in a hyperchange. This is the new world in which our Lord Jesus Christ is building His Church.

> We must become a church that creatively reaches beyond the current barriers to ministry.

As Christ builds His Church, it is our responsibility as His leaders to prepare ourselves so we can have effective ministries, even in these challenging times. But how can we lead effectively in ministry when everything is changing so fast that we feel like it is impossible to keep up? With every passing year, it is becoming more difficult to remain relevant, yet Christ has called us to help build His Church in the midst of this hectic techno-world.

Through the enabling power of the Holy Spirit, we can catapult beyond our cultural challenges. We must become a church that creatively reaches beyond the current barriers to ministry—a church that is a vibrant, holy influence on the new frontier of the twenty-first century—a church of believers who reflect Christ's glory and effectively minister to the spiritually needy imprisoned within the chaotic world system.

Our message is timeless, but it must be presented to people in ways they can understand and will accept. God wants to grow churches that are relevant without compromising biblical truth —churches that know how to connect with the culture around them without forsaking timeless biblical principles. God's Word is as relevant today as it was when God first presented it to humanity; however, we must become effective communicators of that message by staying in touch with our times.

As ministers in this new era, we must constantly reevaluate our ideas and assumptions and their implementation. Unless we do, it will be impossible to be relevant and connect with unbelievers in today's world. We cannot become so comfortable that we ignore the changes that are occurring all around us. We must do this while maintaining the critical balance between innovative thinking and scriptural directives. This is especially important if ministry is to effectively reach a digital generation.

MAPPING THE NEW WORLD

Many years ago, William Edward Perry, the famous English explorer, mapped out most of the Southern Polar Cap. Those who travel to that desolate, subzero continent are still using his maps today. On one particular expedition, he and his crew, having completed mapping an uncharted region, were preparing to hike to another unfamiliar location. On the eve of their departure, they studied the stars and determined their exact coordinates. As the sun rose, they began a hard, lengthy journey north to this unmapped region. They marched through the ice and snow all day long with the freezing air burning their lungs. As the sun set, they made camp, totally exhausted from their trip. After their evening meal, Perry studied the stars again to determine their exact coordinates. He was stunned to learn that even though he and his crew had journeyed north all day, they were now farther south than when they began that morning. After struggling to solve this problem, they discovered that although they had traveled north, they were on a giant ice sheet that was floating south faster than they were walking north. Although they were going in the right direction, they were sliding away and did not even know it.

In which direction are you headed? Many people are marching north with ideas and plans, but sadly, the undercurrent of our shifting culture is pulling them farther away from the realization of their goals. Just like Perry's men, they struggle and press ahead only to find themselves farther and farther away from achieving their ministry objectives.

These are pivotal times in history. The Church is being assailed on all sides by forces strong and dangerous. Eastern religions are sweeping the globe, and pluralism and moral relativity infect all aspects of society, including the church. Like Paul, we understand that we wrestle not against flesh and blood but against supernatural forces (Ephesians 6:12). In these last days, it will take supernatural leadership to pilot the church through these dangerous waters.

It is impossible for the church not to be affected by this powerful shifting taking place because it exists in the culture that is going through the great shift. Many struggle to understand the church's response to this changing world. Should the church embrace this hyperchange and abandon all we are currently doing, or should we remain steadfast in our approaches and structure and prevent change from taking place? Or is the answer somewhere in between? How do we maneuver in the midst of this hyperchange knowing what to keep and what to let go?

In the struggle to remain culturally relevant as well as maintaining the true distinctives of the Christian church, two approaches are dominant. Some have reacted to the change by preferring to preserve who they are more than connecting with the world around them, and have become self-absorbed. Isolating themselves from the changes that are taking place, they build walls that keep the change from affecting them. This is often done with a sincere desire to "keep the faith" and not compromise. The byproduct of this isolation is often a lack of relevance in the form and function of the local church. In the attempt to adhere to the essentials of faith, we may mistakenly perpetuate nonessentials of the faith or, worse, become unaware of the needs of the culture. When we disconnect with the world around us or disconnect with other believers, our isolation prevents us from healthy fellowship and evangelism.

Another approach to the rapidly changing world is to weave the elements of culture into the church activities without adequate discernment. Viewing any change or advancement as a powerful new way to revitalize the church, the emphasis is less on God's direction and more on our own ability to work the cultural shifts to our favor. This methodology can often prevent the church from following God's desires for it, because the church trusts in its own ability and power to advance.

Churches that follow these paths begin with good intentions but are often unwillingly separated from God and the mission they originally set out to accomplish.

The answer is for both sides to find new ways of relating to our shifting culture through new breakthroughs in methodology while remaining grounded in, and supported by, God's timeless foundational principles.

In addition to the polarizing effect of churches either isolating themselves from culture or caving into it, many pastors are not applying the basic truths for supernatural living that are outlined in God's Word. These pastors are committed to pursuing God's purposes but all too often forget to rely on His infinite power and resources. They pray to know God's will, but then when He reveals what He wants them to do, they launch out in their own strength to accomplish the goal. God does not intend us to work independently of Him. He wants us to hold His hand and work together, like Father and child, in accomplishing His task. It is when we let go of His hand and try to do the impossible on our own that frustration sets in and over time can lead to more serious problems.

Notice these alarming trends among many of today's pastors:

- Each month, 1,500 pastors leave the ministry due to moral failure, spiritual burnout, or contention in their church.

- Ninety percent said the ministry was completely different than they thought it would be before they entered ministry.

- Eighty percent of pastors and 84 percent of their spouses feel unqualified and discouraged in their role in ministry.

- Eighty percent of seminary and Bible school graduates who enter the ministry will leave it within the first five years.

- Ninety percent of pastors said their seminary or Bible school training did only a fair to poor job of preparing them for ministry.

- Fifty percent are so discouraged that they would leave the ministry if they could, but have no other way to make a living.

- Seventy percent of pastors do not have a close friend, confidant, or mentor.

- Eighty percent of pastors surveyed spend less than 15 minutes a day in prayer. Ninety-five percent do not regularly pray with their spouse.

- Seventy percent of pastors said the only time they spend studying the Word is when they are preparing sermons.

- Eighty percent of pastors' spouses feel their spouse is overworked.

- Almost 40 percent polled said they had an extramarital affair since beginning their ministry.

- Fifty percent of pastors' marriages will end in divorce.

- Eighty percent of adult children of pastors surveyed have had to seek professional help for depression.[3]

This is a very troubling overview of pastoral ministry. How can pastors be better equipped for the challenges of ministry and cultural changes?

The twenty-first century church must have leaders who are equipped and filled with the Holy Spirit to lead others through these rapidly changing times.

As we survey the new territory before us, we realize it is remarkably different from the land through which we have previously journeyed. We need new maps to guide us. If we are dependent on outdated plans and methods for ministry, we will be ineffective. Future ministry requires leaders who are grounded in the Scriptures and understand the culture around them, but most of all, leaders who are responsive to the guidance of the Holy Spirit. Whether you are a pastor or a lay leader, you must be empowered with supernatural ability to have an effective ministry in this new millennium.

CHANGE OR DIE

It has been said that most people will not change until the price of not changing becomes greater than the cost of the change itself. We must change. If we do not, it will cost us everything. There is no longer any option. Those who cling to outdated methods and practices are becoming obsolete. These groups continue to do the same things they have always done, not because of religious faith or devotion but because they have always done it that way. They lack the real power they claim to possess, and the world sees them as archaic. They refuse to change and eventually will die.

On the other hand, there are those who have abandoned biblical principle in their zeal to be accepted by the culture around them. Consequently, they may achieve increased attendance and popularity, but they are not producing many fruitful disciples for Christ.

If we are not willing to change to meet the needs of those whom God wants to bring to us, we too will die.

For example, imagine an I-beam in your front yard. (An I-beam looks like a capital "I" and is used in construction.) Suppose we lay this I-beam in your front yard, and it stretches to the house across the street. Your neighbors come outside to look in wonder at this 120-foot beam in your street. Imagine that we are standing at the opposite end of the I-beam, 120 feet away, holding a $100 bill. All you have to do is walk across the I-beam in front of your friends, and we will give you the money. Would you come? Of course, you would; it is relatively easy.

If we are not willing to change to meet the needs of those God wants to bring to us, we will die.

Now suppose we move the I-beam to Kuala Lumpur, Malaysia. In Kuala Lumpur, there are two buildings side by side called the Petronas Towers. They are the tallest buildings in the world, standing 1,483 feet tall. This time the I-beam barely bridges the gap between the two buildings. You are on the roof of one building, and we are on the other. "Listen, if you will walk —not crawl—across this I beam in five minutes, we will give you another hundred dollars." Would you do it this time? Probably not. "But it is the same I-beam you crossed yesterday in your front yard! What if I increased the prize to a thousand dollars? What about a million dollars?" Are you still unwilling to take such a risk? Most people value their life more than the money offered to do such a daring feat.

Let us change the circumstances again. This time, standing on the other rooftop are two kidnappers holding your two-year-old daughter. If you do not cross the beam immediately, they will drop your daughter. Now you must decide how important it is to cross the beam. What is more valuable to you? Most people to whom we have presented this scenario say they are willing to attempt the walk. They would not do it for any amount of money, but their love for their child means more and causes them to step out. When the challenge becomes personal, it is amazing how willing people are to take a risk.[4] They are more willing to change when the price of not changing becomes greater than the change itself. How high does the price of changelessness have to become before we will begin to rethink our evangelism strategies and embrace solid, Spirit-filled change today?

We are on the brink of a new world. The I-beam has been laid before us, and the world is dangling in the hands of the enemy. The leadership of the Church is standing on the edge of a great divide. The dangers are incredible; but we remember that though the conditions are different, the I-beam is the same one we traversed yesterday in our front yard.

Unlike in our story, we do not have to cross the beam alone; the Holy Spirit accompanies us as we traverse the narrow rail to the other side. It will be windy and slippery on the journey, but we must work our way across the divide and help save the world from the hands of the enemy.

MAKING THE CHANGE

The first-century church also existed in a world of rapid change. In addition to a radical religious shift from Judaism and paganism to Christianity, the world at that time was going through a massive political upheaval with the advancement of the Roman Empire. Following the establishment of the church on the day of Pentecost, we see that the first-century church, even during its own rapid changes, worked to keep their connection with each other and the world as well as with God. These early believers did not withdraw from the world—they moved into it. Immediately after Pentecost, believers were proclaiming the good news of Jesus Christ to the world (Acts 2:14–36; 3:11–26; 4:1–11). They did not isolate themselves from the world; they sought to evangelize it. Where nonbelievers were found in the Temple, Christians were there. When Jews went to the synagogue, believers were there.

In addition, early believers did not isolate themselves from each other, but devoted themselves to fellowship (Act 2:42). Verse 46 tells us that they continued in one mind in the temple day by day. They worked together in harmony. The walls of separation and isolation were down. Just like the early believers, we are one Body, unified in the Spirit. However, all too often we refuse to work together to accomplish God's purposes. We pursue God's goals but ignore or even reject the principle that we are all different parts of the same body and must work together in harmony for maximum ministry impact.

The first-century church was also centered on God. Acts 2:42 records that Christ's followers devoted themselves to the apostles' teaching. They were devoted to the gospel of Jesus Christ, not wavering in their commitments. The early church is full of examples of the importance of prayer and guidance from God. In the midst of adversity, the church prayed to God for guidance and protection (Acts 4:24–31). When the church was faced with controversy, they sought the direction of God for the answer (Acts 6; Acts 15). They worked in harmony with God for His direction and guidance. Nothing stood as a barrier between their Creator and them.

There has never been a more important time for the Church to follow the pattern of the first-century church and lead a lost world in the right direction. Moral relativism has allowed a sense of irresponsibility to pervade our culture. The ship of culture is adrift in a sea of turmoil and discord. More than ever, leaders are needed to pilot this ship into the peaceful harbor of God's love and grace.

As indicated earlier, this turmoil has affected many church leaders. Consequently, many pastors have not been able to confront the rising tide of depravity, and God's Church is suffering. George Barna, the Christian statistician, recently released his annual study of American faith and religious beliefs. In it he revealed startling trends regarding church members in America: While 82 percent of church members pray, only 37 percent read their Bible outside of church; 41 percent of people who attend church do not consider themselves born again![5] Other studies indicate that 90 percent of church members misunderstand the person and ministry of the Holy Spirit.

Clearly, leaders must help the Christian Church right its course. The only way to combat this rising flood of apathy is through the power of the Holy Spirit. We must have confidence and faith in the power of the Holy Spirit to lead us beyond these limitations. Society and the Church have been gripped with fears about the future. Our rapidly changing world leaves people wondering where we are headed. Too often, these limitations are holding back God's people from being the powerful, fruitful church He has called us to be.

While many in the church shrink back from the changing culture and are oblivious to the assault of the advancing attack of the enemy, it is obvious from Barna's report, and similar studies, that we are in a pivotal time in church history. We must be alert to the change taking place around us and work diligently to turn back the growing tide of evil in the world. Just as leaders like Martin Luther preserved the true gospel during turbulent times, it is necessary for us to rise to the occasion and lead the church in this age of hyperchange.

But we must be clear. It is not enough simply to lead a church; we must lead a church that shines the light of the gospel in a way that balances biblical standards with innovation and theological principle with modernization. Let us draw a clearer picture of such a church—a church with no roof and no walls.

CHAPTER 2

A Church with No Roof and No Walls

From the 1930s through the 1960s, East Africa experienced a great spiritual revival. Thousands of people committed their lives to Jesus Christ during this period of history. Many different missions organizations and national church leaders joined together to be a part of this mighty move of God. One of the themes of this East Africa revival later became the theme for an evangelistic crusade sponsored by Campus Crusade for Christ. The Africans wanted their church to be a "Church with No Roof and a Church with No Walls." A church with no roof has no obstructions to separate it from God's free flow of love, forgiveness, power, and blessings. A church with no walls has no barriers to isolate it from fellow believers in other churches and from those who are without Christ.

Ministry beyond all limits requires "a church with no roof and no walls." A church with no roof and no walls is one that reaches a postmodern cultural context without breaking its commitment to orthodox biblical standards. We believe no other theme can better match our desires for discipleship and evangelism. This is really what the Lord Jesus Christ would have His Church look like. In the early days of Christianity before magnificent cathedrals and massive church structures, the Body of Christ was not defined by its buildings but by its people. In fact, a church that is known more for its steeple than its people is a church known more for its past than its present. We need to move beyond the limitations of our church culture and become more like the apostolic Church of the first century (Acts 2:42). We must remove the things of this world that prevent us from understanding and connecting with God. We also must put aside the differences and divisive issues that keep us from appreciating and joining with others in unified ministry. The more we understand how to be united with God and His awesome power, the more we will be able to be unified with each other.

The African revival revealed something many of us have forgotten as we have tried to advance Christ's gospel. We are to work in harmony with God and with each other so we can fulfill the will of our heavenly Father. We are to be centers of Christ's love and beacons of God's presence to those around us. We must spiritually strive to be a church with no roof and no walls, to minister beyond the limits that have prevented the church from working in unity and harmony with God and man.

SYNERGY IN MINISTRY

The church of the twenty-first century, the church that ministers beyond the limits, is a church that is *synergistic*. What do we mean by synergistic? Synergy is a business term that in recent years has become popular in management and leadership circles. The *Oxford English Dictionary* defines synergy as "joint working, cooperation…that results in increased effectiveness, achievement, etc., produced as a result of combined action or cooperation."[1] The principles of synergy have been in existence from early in history. For centuries, people have worked together to accomplish great tasks that they could not do on their own. The Pyramids and the Great Wall of China were not built by one individual, but by many people working together. It took the combined effort of everyone involved to achieve the goal. It took synergy.

In *Seven Habits of Highly Effective People*, Stephen Covey defines the sixth habit, synergy, as "the sum is greater than the whole."[2] However, this only begins to explain the nuances of "synergy," especially as it relates to the Church. God created us to live and work in harmony with Him and others in the Body of Christ. As we do, He multiplies the results of our combined efforts. He takes the loaves and fish we bring Him and uses them to accomplish the impossible (Matthew 14:13–21). Every person has been entrusted with gifts and resources that are vital to the well-being of Christ's Church (Romans 12:6–21). As a result, we are all equal and important members of a team. Synergy is developed as each person contributes to the whole. In Covey's words, "The sum product from the team is much greater than the sum total of all the individual achievements."[3]

Synergistic churches are dynamic, living bodies of believers. They work cohesively together to achieve the goals that Christ lays before them just like the various parts of the human body work together to carry out daily activities. Every person in the church—from top to bottom—works together to help fulfill the Great Commission. People must first work in synergy with God, their Creator, and then with each other. God provides the direction and guidance while the team of believers serves as the resources and manpower God uses. He uses us as we make ourselves available to Him.

Synergy provides an important energy that helps to propel the ministry of the local church. Jesus prayed in John 17:21 "that they may all be one; even as Thou, Father, art in Me, and I in Thee." Unity is not something believers work to attain; rather, unity in the nature of the Church. It is a spiritual benefit of a believer's relationship to Christ, the Head. This is why Paul encourages us to "preserve" the unity of the Church and not create an or manufacture it (Ephesians 4:3).

Synergy is closely related to unity. Christ's desire for His disciples was not only that they would be one in the Holy Spirit, but also that they would achieve more together than they could accomplish alone. Synergy is this dynamic that occurs among a local body of believers who are dedicated to walking together in the unity of Christ. A synergistic church is one that is committed to practical implementation of Christ's prayer in John 17:21, and, as a consequence of that commitment, enjoys the fruit of multiplied effectiveness.

The synergistic church advances the kingdom of God with greater effectiveness because it utilizes every member and all its resources to the maximum potential. It is a church focused on bringing people together with Christ and with each other. Synergy is formed and strengthened through relationships. The priority of synergistic churches is to disciple believers and help them develop a committed, growing relationship with Jesus Christ and then to form strong relationships with other believers. This exemplifies the community of faith Jesus Christ desires. When we are part of a community that values one another, the lost are attracted to Christ's kingdom. Everybody is a somebody in the Body of Christ.

People-Centered, Not Program-Driven

Relationships require one key ingredient—people. The church of the twenty-first century is not only made up of people, it is focused on people. Synergy requires the cultivation of relationships that produce trust and accountability. This involves more than small-group meetings or clever programs. It requires a continual emphasis on encouraging people to connect with God and each other. A synergistic church is people-centered because it is Christ-centered. Jesus came to save people and build strong relationships while He was on earth. We must develop our programs based on the needs of people. The church exists for the purpose of ministering to people.

In the past, churches have been tempted to emphasize events and programs more than people. A successful church may have a strong bus ministry, Vacation Bible Schools, day care, youth activities, or whatever the popular program of the day might be. This is not to devalue the importance of quality programs and events, for they are necessary parts of the local church. If we are not careful, however, the program becomes more important than the people coming to the program. Programs are justifiable only as long as they meet the needs of the people who attend them. As members of the Body of Christ, we must make the people of the church one of our top priorities. Christ cared enough for people that He died on the cross for their sins. We should care enough about people to introduce them to our Savior and help them grow in Him.

> **The synergistic church is focused on bringing people together with Christ and with each other.**

The new generations of Gen Xers and Millennials do not appreciate a program-centered church. They are looking for authentic, experiential faith that meets them where they are and allows them to be a part of a greater spiritual picture. They need a place to connect and belong so they can receive from God and others. This is where the synergistic church can meet the needs of a new generation. Synergistic churches do not just have events or programs for the program's sake. They structure what they are doing to meet people's needs and fulfill their God-given mission. They understand that people are important to God; therefore, people must be important to the church.

Interdependence vs. Independence

Synergy is achieved through the Holy Spirit, who enables us to work interdependently with each other. To truly achieve synergy, the leadership and members of the church must live their lives under the principle of interdependence. It is important to understand the impact of this concept on the "beyond all limits" church. To achieve interdependent synergy, openness and authenticity are required. Unbiblical power structures and struggles must be left behind, and biblical paradigms of teamwork and trust must be embraced. Leadership and authority are shared with the team, empowering every part of the church to be active in the mission of the church. The synergistic church emphasizes interdependence, not religious hierarchy.

This synergistic approach utilizes the God-given gifts of each member of the church. This is true within the local church as well as in the Church universal. Synergistic churches carry the interdependence from their own church to the community. The spirit of competition gives way to the spirit of cooperation as the Body of Christ works together to reach its community, providing vital assistance to the needy and leadership to the city.

The days of territorialism and "sheep stealing" are long gone. Bob Reccord, President of the Southern Baptist Mission Board, shared with over fifty pastors of different denominations that the church of the future, the synergistic church, will be a church "where logos and egos are left at the door." It will not be concerned with personal advancement and prestige. What is most important is that people are being transformed by Christ. The independent spirit of Christian mavericks creates Christian hermits in a world where networking has become vitally important.

NEW LEADERS FOR A NEW TIME

The greatest asset for building the synergistic church is strong leadership. Paul writes, "He gave some as apostles, and some as ers for the equipping of the saints for the work of service, to the building up of the body of Christ" (Ephesians 4:11,12). One of the most important people in any community is a Spirit-filled pastor. One of the greatest assets to any city is the presence of a pastor who hears from God and is not afraid to act in obedience. The greatest assets to any church are believers who are filled with the Holy Spirit and are committed to working together for the cause of Jesus Christ. The synergistic church is filled with laity, pastors, church leaders, evangelists, missionaries, and counselors who are working in harmony with God's direction and in cooperation with each other.

This key component of the church and the community is often overlooked. Church leaders are typically underpaid and under-appreciated. They face spiritual battles in addition to the normal challenges of everyday life. We value each of these pastors highly and pray earnestly that God would bless and anoint them for a ministry that is even more effective than before. God did not intend for them to wander powerless and alone in the harvest field to which He called them. The future of the church is in the hands of its present leaders. They must determine now what kind of leader they will be—independent mavericks or synergistic leaders. They need to know who they are in Christ and why God has called them into ministry.

The church of the future will need leaders who are constantly being changed into the image of Christ. They must live in humility before God and submit themselves to the Holy Spirit's direction. The synergistic church will need leaders who live interdependently in their communities. In fact, Jesus taught that the one who seeks to be a leader must be a servant of all.

The Importance of Leadership

John Maxwell has said, "Everything rises and falls on leadership."[4] We cannot agree more. Barriers will be encountered by every church leader. Leaders must break through these barriers and limitations that have handcuffed the growth of their church. These barriers will become the stepping stones to greatness when overcome through faith and determination. Great leaders focus on the value and purpose of trials, not the pain.

Despite the seemingly insurmountable barriers, we believe the greatest days of the church are ahead. Statisticians report that there are more people coming to Christ every day than ever before. The future of a church rests in the strength of its leaders. If the leadership is inadequate, the church will not prosper. If the leadership simply maintains, then the church will never progress. However, if the leadership of the church is determined to move forward, then the church will also grow. We must know the difference between having a "cause" and having a vision for our lives and ministries. A God-inspired vision is worth living for, but a God-given cause is worth dying for. Jesus said, "If anyone wishes to come after Me, he must deny himself, and take up his cross and follow Me" (Mark 8:34). We must be committed to a cause worth getting up for every day, something worth dying for.

We must know the difference between having a "cause" and having a vision for our ministries.

Many books are available on leadership and management. In fact, *Beyond All Limits* joins a growing list of books for Christian leaders. However, this is not a book on how to do leadership. This book is about *be*-ing, not *do*-ing. After years of ministry (Bill 55, James 25), it has become clear that *one must be something before one can do something*. We have also discovered that *one must be something before one can say something*. This book will not give quick-fix steps to implement in your church to experience church growth. The distinctives of the synergistic

Information Age engulfs us. George Gilder, in his futuristic book *The Telecosm*, states that information and the speed with which that information is reaching us double every six months.[5] This means more information can be sent in a second over a single cable than was sent over the entire Internet in one month in 1997. Bombarded by competing voices, people are not looking for information givers; they are looking for someone to help them use that information to take them where they long to be. They are looking for a leader.

Becoming an effective leader is a lifelong journey, not a singular event. It is a process of spiritual transformation that takes place every day in the life of a follower of Jesus Christ. That transformation is begun in us by Christ and continues every day of our lives through the power of the Holy Spirit (Philippians 1:6).

The apostle Paul lived the life of a synergistic leader. Paul had been to all the right schools, was an expert in the Law and the Prophets, was a friend of the disciples, and even saw a vision of Christ; yet he submitted himself to the process of daily transformation. This apostle, who had seen the risen Christ on the Damascus Road, realized the necessity of dying daily (Galatians 2:2). He was dependent upon the Spirit of God to transform him into who he needed to become in Christ. While his physical body was experiencing the aging process, his inner man was being renewed every day (2 Corinthians 4:16). Reliance on Jesus Christ and a willingness to be led by the Holy Spirit made Paul a powerful servant leader.

In Galatians 5:16–26, Paul revealed the fruits of the Spirit, which are also the fruits of successful ministry: love, joy, peace, patience, kindness, goodness, faithfulness, gentleness, and self-control. A present-day leader's ministry depends on the Spirit's guidance just as Paul's did. Even Paul, who wrote a significant portion of the New Testament, needed the daily guidance of the

Spirit. Paul's ministry effectiveness was directly proportionate to the health of his relationship with God.

The Synergistic Leader

The distinctives of the synergistic church must also be embraced by the leadership of that church. Too many times, those in church leadership do not differentiate between their own spiritual walk with God and their church work. If the church is going well, then their spiritual life is going well. If the church is struggling, then they are struggling. It is obvious that these two areas of the minister's life may be related, but they are not equal. All who are called upon to lead God's people must be wholly committed to Jesus Christ. They must *be* something before they *do* something. When we assume that our hard work and effort are the equivalent of devotion and humility before God, we make a grave mistake. It is then that we focus more on *doing* than *being*. It is a faith that is lived with our hands but not found in our hearts. There is no synergy with God as we minister. We work *for* Him rather than *with* Him. We work independently rather than inviting Him to live in us and through us.

Others are so task-oriented that they do not have time to actually relate to the people to whom they are ministering. New converts are just another "notch on their spiritual gun." These people constantly compare the numbers of people in attendance or the size of their latest event with other churches and pastors. Conversations with these people always revolve around the three B's: buildings, budgets, and bodies. It almost seems that a larger sanctuary, a bigger budget, and more bodies have greater importance than relationships or life change in their congregations. Sadly, these kinds of leaders seek to achieve a celebrity status because of pride and arrogance. They view themselves as apart from the common believer, thinking they are in a different "class" because of the ministry they have built. They lack the

~~Church of Jesus Christ. They will not be able to continue this~~ prima donna attitude on the new frontier of ministry.

People today desire leaders to whom they can relate—those who are real and who serve in humility before Christ; those who are not afraid to reveal their weaknesses, knowing that others will work with them to compensate for their deficiencies. They know that in return they will help others to utilize the many talents and gifts God has given them. These leaders are necessary for the growth and health of the church.

It is these kinds of leaders who have the confidence to work together with other leaders to reach their communities for Christ. Synergistic leaders are not consumed with "territories" and denominationalism but with reaching the lost for Christ. They trust God to guide them as they build the synergistic church on the new frontier. It is a frontier that takes them far beyond anything they can ask or even imagine. It is a ministry that is truly beyond all limits.

THE BLUEPRINT FOR THE SYNERGISTIC CHURCH

In Chapter 1, we surveyed the new world that is in transition around us. We discussed the necessity of changing how we see the world and the importance of understanding the Information Age in which we live. We believe the church God is building for the future is a church that is built upon the principle of synergy. While each church is unique, all must work together to meet the needs of ministry in a changing world. It may be a challenge for some to abandon old forms and ingrained traditions. Unlike many strategies for ministry, we will not highlight the six steps to building a church or the three necessary programs that will make your church grow. These kinds of "secret steps of church growth will not help in the twenty-first century. The principles and plans that have made one church grow may not work in another church. The diversity that has resulted from the digital world and globalization creates new challenges for churches. The needs of a church in Collegeville, Arkansas (population 200), will be different from Los Angeles, California (population over 3 million). That is why this book is not a quick fix to church growth. There are no shortcuts to true growth. Only God can build the Church and draw men and women to Himself.

Through the years, we have observed that the churches that apply the principles of synergy see the most growth. Though their needs and strategies are different, these churches all have common distinctives that enable them to be effective lighthouses in their communities. The distinctives are not exhaustive nor the answer for every problem churches will face. They are by no means the be-all and end-all of planting and growing a church, but they are vitally important to the fulfillment of Christ's mandate to advance the gospel.

The crusade in East Africa provided us a slogan that illustrates the genius of the synergistic church. The "beyond all limits" church is a church with no roof and no walls. Just as on the day of Pentecost, the fire of heaven can fall upon us because there is no roof to block its descent and the wind of the Spirit can blow across us because there are no walls to hinder its flow. It is our prayer that God will spark the flames of revival in every church and spread it by the wind of the Holy Spirit!

A Church with No Roof

The East African church understood that the most important aspect of any church is its vital connection with God. When the roof is off, nothing blocks the Spirit of God from moving in and among His people. It experienced a massive revival that swept much of Africa for many years because of the connection with

God. T'
dered
charac
church mu.

Beyond Fear and Self-Reli.   .e

The church without a proper understanding of who God is and how He works in our lives is limited in its impact in this world. Without the assurance of the sovereign work of God, we are left to take the ministry of Christ into our own hands and rely on our own power to accomplish the will of God. Worse yet, we can become so afraid of the result of our actions that we never do anything. World events such as the destruction of the World Trade Center and the rise of terrorism cause fear to grip the world and even the church when we do not trust in God. Some are prevented from moving forward because of fear of the unknown. Both of these limitations, self-reliance and fear, stem from a misunderstanding of who God is and where we place our confidence. When we do not place our faith and trust in an all-powerful God who desires to bless us because of His unfailing love, we are forced to step out in our own strength or not step out at all. Paul writes to Timothy in 2 Timothy 1:7, "God has not given us a spirit of timidity, but of power and love and discipline." We know that we have nothing to fear because *when the roof is off, we place our confidence in God.* We can see Him at work on our behalf, and we respond to Him in faith. We know He is working in us to do the work He has called us to do. Scripture tells us to, "Trust in the Lord with all your heart, and do not lean on your own understanding. In all your ways acknowledge Him, and He will make your paths straight" (Proverbs 3:5,6). By having a clearer understanding of God's magnificent attributes, we do not rely on our own strength but trust in Him to provide for us. We reflect His glory to the world as we learn more and more

41

about who God is. As a result, we trust in God's character, rely on His Word for guidance, and depend on His Spirit to empower us to live holy lives.

Beyond Doubt and Uncertainty

Laurie Beth Jones, in her book *The Path*, states that the number one fear of people is having lived a meaningless life.[6] In the midst of change, a sense of uncertainty plagues the church and the world. This uncertainty has caused many to doubt the work they are doing or doubt the things they thought were true. James 1:6 tells us that "the one who doubts is like the surf of the sea driven and tossed by the wind." When we doubt our calling, we cannot persevere in the ministry because we lack the assurance of knowing that we are really called to do what we are doing. Researchers tell us that the average length of stay for pastors is continually decreasing. Church leaders are leaving the ministry every day because they question their calling.

The call of God upon the lives of ministers is the anchor that gives them stability.

As the world changes rapidly around us, it is important that ministers of the gospel do not let uncertainty and doubt influence them. Those who minister for Christ must know they are called to preach the gospel. *When the roof is off, we trust in the calling of God.* Unfortunately, there are too many people attempting to lead the church who have never been called to do so. The call of God upon the lives of ministers is the anchor that gives them stability as the rest of the world crumbles. Because of their calling, Jeremiah, Isaiah, and Ezekiel could each trust in the message they were delivering despite the attacks of their enemies and the lack of response from their hearers (Jeremiah 1; Isaiah 6; Ezekiel 3).

Jesus did not begin His earthly ministry until after He had fasted and sought His Father's face for forty days. There is no better way to determine God's call. If you are in doubt of your calling, follow the Lord's example. It is imperative that all leaders understand the nature and power of their ministerial calling. We can trust in this calling when trials and setbacks occur for we know we have a divine commission.

Beyond Hypocrisy and Unfaithfulness

The world is looking for people who live consistent, godly lives. Most individuals are aware of their own shortcomings. They look to others who can model, as well as preach, holy living. Sadly, the church world has often neglected modeling faith as well as preaching faith. Hypocrisy has long been a deserved accusation against the church. We cannot allow our effectiveness to be limited by an inability to live like Jesus wants us to live. Synergistic churches minister beyond the limits of hypocrisy and unfaithfulness. *When the roof is off, our character is constantly being molded into the image of Christ.* Christ works in us to develop this character. Romans 12:1,2 admonishes us to be transformed by God. Later, in Romans 12:9, we are commanded to love without hypocrisy, living consistent lives. As His vessels, we are open to God, and He shapes us into what we need to be and who we need to become through Him. He transforms us as the potter transforms lumps of clay into works of art. He helps us to overcome sin in our lives and gives us the strength to fulfill the ministry He calls us to do. In saving His harshest words for religious leaders whose character did not match their words, Jesus taught that one of the greatest mistakes of ministry is to misrepresent the gospel through an unfaithful, hypocritical lifestyle. The synergistic leader is a leader whose character is in harmony with Christ.

Beyond Self-Centeredness and Idolatry

The life of faith is a life that is devoted to God. When we acknowledge Jesus Christ as our Lord and Savior, we are committed to following Him as His disciple. Discipleship requires us to obey Christ's commands. Disobedience reveals our self-centeredness and lack of devotion. By placing our own needs or desires before Christ's commands, we fall victim to a form of idolatry. Titus 1:15,16 says, "To the pure all things are pure; but to those who are defiled and unbelieving, nothing is pure, but both their mind and their conscience are defiled. They profess to know God but by their deeds they deny Him, being detestable and disobedient and worthless for any good deed." *When the roof is off, synergistic churches demonstrate wholehearted commitment to God.* We demonstrate our commitment to God by communicating with Him through prayer and fasting (Acts 13:3; 14:23). We also demonstrate our commitment to God by focusing our lives and thoughts on Him through praise and worship (Luke 24:53; Acts 2:47), as well as by aggressively pursuing the fulfillment of the Great Commission (Matthew 28:19,20).

A lack of devotion will limit the connection we have with God because we value ourselves and other things as being more important than God (1 Samuel 15:1–23). This violates the very foundations of our faith. When we live a life of commitment, we move beyond the limits of our own shortcomings. In order to pastor a "beyond all limits" church, we must be willing to allow the wind of the Holy Spirit to blow our roofs off.

A Church with No Walls

The African church experienced revival because its walls were down. The synergistic church does not keep God's presence inside. It is not enough simply to receive God's presence; we must share Him with the world around us. We are a church that has no walls. We biblically and practically approach the community around us to create a center of refreshing and power. We are open to the eyes of the world, modeling before them the Spirit-filled life that results from the roof being off. We are acting as salt and light to the world. The walls that once held us in have fallen and now serve as bridges to the world around us. We represent real, authentic faith, and invite the world to come and join in our worship of the Creator. The synergistic church is in the middle of the marketplace, working and growing as a beacon of hope to those who are in need of it. The openness of the synergistic church is seen and felt through four distinctives: cooperation, communication, compassion, and creativity. Each distinctive helps the church move beyond limitations it faces.

Beyond Jealousy and Isolationism

It is sad that for too long the church has been known for isolationism and jealousy rather than cooperation. Many churches and pastors view themselves as small kingdoms that compete with other rival churches for people and profits. When God moves in one church, other churches often do not rejoice in God's outpouring of blessing but ridicule them and become jealous. These limitations have prevented churches from efficiently reaching their communities and modeling the love for each other that Christ commanded. Synergistic churches are not afraid to partner with other churches and groups because they live beyond the limits of isolation and jealousy. We must not be concerned with "who gets the converts" or whether "my church is bigger than your church!" We must work together in love and humility as we preach the gospel.

This kind of unity in spirit was what Paul prayed would happen in the Philippian church:

> If therefore there is any encouragement in Christ, if there is any consolation of love, if there is any fellowship of the Spirit, if any affection and compassion, make my joy

complete by being of the same mind, maintaining the same love, united in spirit, intent on one purpose. Do nothing from selfish or empty conceit, but with humility of mind let each of you regard one another as more important than himself; do not merely look out for your own personal interests, but also for the interests of others (Philippians 2:1–4).

When the walls are down, the church cooperates with those around them. The principles of synergy and interdependence should mark every avenue of church life. We serve each other in humility knowing that when we do, we model the attitude of Christ (Philippians 2:5–8). Synergistic churches find ways to model cooperation across racial, economic, denominational, and social lines. The walls have come down and the bricks that have fallen are used to build bridges to unite us. While it is easier to build fences than bridges, we must be willing to exchange our personal, manmade fences for God-given bridges to a world without hope or truth.

Beyond Ambiguity and Irrelevance

Communication is vital to the life of the twenty-first century church. Never before have we experienced such an explosion of information. Technology has increased the number of people in the world who are talking to one another. Direct broadcast systems have brought an unimaginable number of television and radio channels into every home. Mobile technology has allowed email and wireless services to be accessible to most everyone. The number of "voices" the average person hears has increased. The church's voice and message must be clear and relevant as we make our way into the new century, speaking to the world around us. Paul reminds us, "If the trumpet produces an uncertain sound, who will prepare himself for battle?" (1 Corinthians 14:8). Our message must be understandable to everyone.

When the walls are down, the church demonstrates effective communication. The synergistic leader and the synergistic church give a clear message. The greatest truths die in the minds of those who cannot articulate them. If we do not preach the message to the lost, they will never hear the message of the gospel. If they do not hear, they will not be able to believe (Romans 10:14). While the world is awash with many unclear, ambiguous sounds demanding attention, the church must sound a clear call of repentance that speaks to the heart of the culture around it.

Beyond Apathy and Insensitivity

Those who need a helping hand should not have to turn to the government for assistance but should find the church to be a place where they can receive physical and spiritual healing. The church should also be active in love. The Church of Jesus Christ is the recipient of the greatest gift of compassion and love the world has ever seen. It was because God loved us that He gave His Son to die for us (John 3:16). As recipients of God's love and compassion, we must reflect that love to the world as well. An apathetic church does not care what is going on around it, forgetting that it was love that first brought its members to Christ. It is more concerned about its own needs than the needs of others. We must pray that God will remove our insensitivity to the hurts of others and make us aware of community needs. "If a brother or sister is without clothing and in need of daily food, and one of you says to them, 'Go in peace, be warmed and be filled,' and yet you do not give them what is necessary for their body, what use is that?" (James 2:15,16). We must minister the love of Christ beyond the limitations of apathy and insensitivity. *When the walls are down, the church is filled with heartfelt compassion.* In fact, it is this compassion for a hurting world that contributed to the fall of these walls. Compassion motivates us to carry the good news of the gospel to those who are lost. It forces us to value the families who make up our churches and plan ways to strengthen them. It is through "compassion ministries" that we make a significant impact on today's society. As believers, we are to be devoted to each other in love while at the same time not forgetting those who are in need around us (Romans 12:10,16).

Beyond Inflexibility and Closed-Mindedness

For the church to continue to be a powerful voice in its community, it must stay on the cutting edge of creativity. While the message of the gospel is sharp and powerful, we must not present it in outdated, ineffective forms (Hebrews 4:12). We cannot expect the methods of yesterday to hold fast today when the world around us has changed so rapidly. We must use the latest in technology to make our message relevant and timely. We are not bound by old paradigms but must constantly strive to be on the cutting edge. Those who choose to be close-minded and inflexible have not heeded the words of Jesus: "No one puts new wine into old wineskins; otherwise the new wine will burst the skins, and it will be spilled out, and the skins will be ruined" (Luke 5:37). The synergistic church ministers beyond the limitations of inflexibility and close-mindedness. *When the walls are down, the church is on the cutting-edge of creativity.* The church that is ineffective in communicating the gospel must adapt its methods to the changing culture. Inflexibility prevents the church from moving forward with statements like, "We have never done it that way before." Through creativity, synergistic leaders must focus their minds to achieve innovation and spur imagination.

> Those who choose to be close-minded and inflexible have not heeded the words of Jesus.

A CHURCH THAT MODELS
INTERDEPENDENCE

The synergistic church and its leadership create a greater value by working together than by working independently. Their interdependence enables them to accomplish the tasks Christ entrusted to them. Through their confidence, calling, character, and commitment, they are able to move beyond the limitations of fear, self-reliance, doubt, uncertainty, hypocrisy, unfaithfulness, self-centeredness, and idolatry because the roof is off their church. Through cooperation, communication, compassion, and creativity, they are able to move beyond the limitations of apathy, insensitivity, ambiguity, irrelevance, jealousy, isolationism, inflexibility, and close-mindedness because the walls are down in their church.

The eight distinctives mentioned above work together to create an effective pulpit ministry, as depicted in the illustration on the following page. These distinctives of the synergistic church are not new or unique. In fact, many of these characteristics are seen in action in your ministry and church. However, we all must focus our lives and energies on the task of helping to fulfill the Great Commission in the twenty-first century. For over fifty years, Campus Crusade for Christ has partnered with churches from every continent and every major denomination as well as thousands of missions groups. It is the Holy Spirit who has enabled us to be a part of so many different ministries and still maintain the essentials of biblical faith. Our mission is still true: to serve the Church of Jesus Christ as it evangelizes and disciples the world. The vast assortment of leaders and churches with whom we have partnered are represented in this book. It is a colloquy of experiences from the ministries of Cutting Edge International and Campus Crusade for Christ.

These distinctives become the bedrock for building a "beyond all limits" church. They are discussed in detail in the following chapters. As you read, write down ideas and thoughts that challenge you. Capitalize on the concepts the Holy Spirit births in you by making them a part of your own spiritual journey as well as your church's. We pray that your life will be lived in synergistic harmony as the Spirit of God allows you to live your life in a church that has "no roof and no walls."

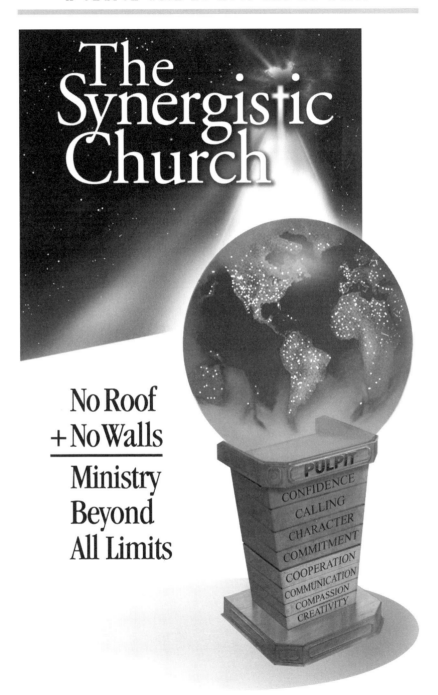

The Synergistic Church

No Roof
+ No Walls
_____
Ministry
Beyond
All Limits

PULPIT

CONFIDENCE
CALLING
CHARACTER
COMMITMENT
COOPERATION
COMMUNICATION
COMPASSION
CREATIVITY

PART ONE

A Church with No Roof

CHAPTER 3

Confidence in God

J esus Christ gave the most effective strategy for church growth over 2,000 years ago. While teaching His disciples, He told them, "I will build my Church and the gates of Hell will not prevail against it" (Matthew 16:18). True church growth is when Jesus Christ builds His Church by drawing people to Himself. Speaking of His death, He said, "If I be lifted up from the earth, I will draw all men unto me" (John 12:32, KJV). Despite the problems the world is facing today and in spite of the enormous challenges and struggles the evangelical church must overcome, God is still building His Church. The essential element of the synergistic church is the realization that God is in control of all that we do and all that we are. We must be centered on God as a church, as a body, and as individuals.

While others may doubt the future and run from the many adversities that come our way, we have confidence—faith—that we can continue in the mission we have been called to accomplish because of our relationship with our sovereign, all-powerful, loving God and Savior. We can live and grow beyond the limits of fear and disappointment because we have faith in the God whom we serve. We have faith in His Word to guide us through the new territories into which He is leading us. We have faith that His Spirit will enable us to move into new depths of His love.

This confidence in God enables anyone to fulfill his or her calling in life. It enables us to know that God, the grand architect of the Church, is working today to build His Church through us. If we will be diligent to hear His voice and lift Him up before all of humanity, He will continue to draw them to Himself. This synergistic approach—God working in and through us—is the only way the Church will ever be truly built on a solid foundation beyond the limits that now restrict the church's impact. The synergistic church and its leadership rely upon God to guide them by His Spirit and His Word. We work in harmony with Him as we travel the course He has charted before us.

CONFIDENCE IN GOD BASED UPON HIS CHARACTER

Many years ago Dr. James Montgomery Boice of the *Bible Hour* radio program interviewed me for his radio show. One of the first questions he asked was, "Dr. Bright, what is the most important truth to teach any follower of Christ?" No one had ever asked me a question like that before, and I was not sure what to answer. Then the Holy Spirit answered through me, "The attributes of God." Many years have passed since that interview, but the realization never left me that understanding God and His attributes were the most important things any believer can know. It launched a journey of discovery and learning about God that resulted in my book *GOD: Discover His Character*. We are more convinced than ever that there is nothing more important to teach believers than the attributes of God. Everything about our lives—our attitudes, motives, dreams, actions, words, perceptions, literature, music, and interaction with others—is influenced by our view of God. We react to the situations of life based upon our beliefs about God. If we have a wrong view, it leads to problems in every other part of our life. It also affects the lives of everyone we influence. Leaders define their ministry through understanding who God is, what God does, and where God leads them. It gives faith and confidence for the race ahead. When we start with the Creator of the universe, our magnificent God who is worthy of all glory and worship, how can we fail?

How big is your God? If you had to explain Him to an unbeliever, what words would you use to describe Him? No one can completely understand the full complexity or impact of God's nature and essence. If humanity could fully understand God, He would not be God; however, we are convinced that the defining reality of any person's life is their knowledge of and personal relationship with the God of the Bible.

Creating an Accurate Picture of God

Our picture of God dictates how we understand and relate to God. In his best-selling book *Knowing God*, J. I. Packer states, "The ignorance of God—ignorance both of His ways and of the practice of communion with Him—lies at the root of much of the church's weakness."[1] As leaders, we must know God not only for ourselves but also to be able to teach others about Him. The Christian life is a walk of faith, and that which is not of faith is sin. "Without faith it is impossible to please [God]" (Hebrews 11:6), but our faith must have an object. The size of our faith will be determined by our understanding of the one in whom we choose to place our faith, for our faith is no greater than its object. If we choose to place our faith in ourselves, our faith will be restricted by our limitations; therefore, we must learn to place our faith in the God of the Bible.

As we meditate on His greatness, God's attributes will inspire us to trust Him for greater things, for "as [a man] thinks within himself, so he is" (Proverbs 23:7). The more we meditate on the love and the wonder of our great God and Savior, the more our own self-centered thoughts are replaced. The right perception of God forces us to evaluate our lives and reach out to the world with the message of Jesus Christ. Ignorance of who God is and how we commune with Him weakens the walk of faith. Leaders must not be ignorant of these vital truths.

We can only gain a correct view of God by studying His attributes and His character. The study of God is an adventure that lasts a lifetime. No one book, much less one chapter in a book, can fully represent all the aspects of the God of the universe. We suggest you begin the journey with the book *GOD: Discover His Character*. Let it be the beginning of a lifelong passion to know God. Study what the Bible says about Him, meditate on His attributes, and see His sovereign hand at work in your life. Become like Paul who wanted only to "know Him and the power of His resurrection" (Philippians 3:10). God is real. He is present everywhere and full of unlimited power and majesty; therefore, we must study and meditate on His marvelous nature.

Have you ever wondered what God looks like? When Michelangelo painted the Sistine Chapel, he struggled with painting the face of God. Throughout history, artists have rendered God in a variety of ways, but all lack the true awareness of the real God of the universe. The picture of God that we have in our hearts and minds establishes the way we live our lives. Those who view God as a mean disciplinarian who meddles in the affairs of helpless humanity are often judgmental and have problems with authority. If we view God as a happy Santa Claus figure who only loves and forgives His children, we assume He will not hold us responsible and accountable for our sinful actions because He is so loving. If we view God as a heavenly bellman running to and fro throughout the universe to meet our needs, we will most likely abuse His goodness and grace. None of these common perceptions of God is true.

In the study of God, we must realize that the human mind is incapable of fully grasping the totality of God. Our finiteness limits our understanding of the infinite. We must be careful not to have a human-centered view of God lest we limit the ability of God to work in our lives. Everything in this world, even the universe, is finite. Only God is infinite. The prophet Isaiah wrote, "Who has measured the waters in the hollow of His hand, and marked off the heavens by the span, and calculated the dust of the earth by the measure, and weighed the mountains in a balance and the hills in a pair of scales? Who has directed the Spirit of the LORD, or as His counselor has informed Him?" (40:12,13). His infinite nature means He has no limits or boundaries. Each of His attributes—love, holiness, mercy, justice, goodness, etc.—are also infinite. They are unlimited in their scope and expression.

> The picture of God that we have in our hearts and minds establishes the way we live our lives.

We also see that God is self-existent. God was not "created." He exists outside the created plan and order of this world. When we "create" something, we rework existing materials to "create" something new. He created the universe out of nothing and He exists apart from it; therefore, He is wholly different and independent of His creation. God is also eternal. Time for humanity has a beginning and an end. We use time to mark periods of history, special occasions, and even future events. They all have a beginning and an end. God, however, is not bound to a "space-time" continuum. He exists eternally. God experiences all the events of history simultaneously—past, present, and future. This means that what God does in history is also impacting history. When Jesus Christ of Nazareth, God in human form, died on the cross over two thousand years ago, He died for all of humanity—past, present, and future.

Not only is God infinite, He is also self-sufficient. Without food, water, and oxygen, all living things on earth die. God is a living being, but He is not dependent upon outside assistance for sufficiency. God is not vulnerable nor does He need help in any way. At times, His planning and sovereignty allow individuals to participate in His activities, but He is not dependent upon them. We can approach God in faith, knowing that nothing is impossible for the One who can do all things.

In the study of the nature of God, it is important to understand that all of His attributes, qualities, and characteristics are interrelated. We cannot understand them separate from each other and fully appreciate them. For the sake of study, it is necessary to isolate these concepts; but in God's economy, they are all working together in cohesion, allowing His character to be fully expressed to humanity.

God, the All-Powerful Creator

God is the Creator of all things. He spoke the unfathomable vastness of our universe into existence and laid the foundations of the world. We see His power and divine nature through His creation. This creative power alone is enough for people not to have any excuse for not knowing and worshiping their Creator. Leaders know that the God they serve is the originator of all things, and this provides assurance regarding the planning and execution of the leadership to which God has called us. Because God has created everything, we trust His ability to work in our lives. His ability to create assures us of His ability to sustain.

We do not serve a weak God! We serve the God who spoke, and the sun and more than 100 billion galaxies came into existence. He waved His hand across an empty sky, and an array of stars filled the night. Each star is the representative of a solar system light-years from earth, full of unknown planets and moons.

His power in creation is evidenced every night we look up and see the billions of stars that cover the heavens.

Because God is a creating God, the synergistic church understands that its work and ministry are birthed in the heart of God. It is God who begins the work and builds His Church. As stewards of the work God creates, we do not own the church. It is God's responsibility to grow the church as we follow in obedience to His direction. We respond to His creative power in worship and trust. We know that the same hand of God that separated the dry land from the waters and molded the first man from clay created us. The God of creation knows everything that takes place in the lives of His creation and works on our behalf. We can trust that God will not fail us just as He did not fail in creating the world. Any problem we face as leaders is insignificant compared to the challenge of creating and maintaining the universe.

Not only did God create the world, but He also remains in control of the world. His power is revealed not only in His Son, Jesus Christ (1 Corinthians 1:24), but also in the order of the universe. Everything has its purpose and its place, and He upholds and maintains it by the power of His Word (Hebrews 1:3). Without God's unique control in the world, all would be chaos. This sovereign control must be understood in the balance of all of His attributes, and all the attributes of God must be viewed together in order to have an accurate picture of God. His sovereignty must be viewed in light of His justice, compassion, love, and mercy. For example, God is not a tyrant who reigns over the world with an iron fist. His love and compassion prevent Him from such unholy uses of power and control.

Because of the sovereignty of God, we understand He is the omniscient ruler of the universe who rules in holiness and goodness. God is the source of all truth and knows everything that can ever be known. He never learns anything. He is not shocked at the course of human events or surprised at the actions of mankind. Only He knows everything about humanity and history. When we go to God in prayer, we are not informing God of our needs for He already knows them, but we show our dependence upon Him by taking our needs to the God who knows all the answers. "The eyes of the LORD are in every place, watching the evil and the good" (Proverbs 15:3). "The LORD looks from heaven; He sees all the sons of men; from His dwelling place He looks out on all the inhabitants of the earth, He who fashions the hearts of them all, He who understands all their works" (Psalm 33:13–15).

We lead knowing that we may be piloting the ship, but it is God who is moving the ship forward.

God is omnipotent. Daniel tells us that "it is He who changes the times and the epochs; He removes kings and establishes kings; He gives wisdom to wise men and knowledge to men of understanding" (2:21). Because He is the Creator, He stays in control. Jeremiah uses the image of a potter's wheel to describe the control God has over creation. The hands of the potter (God) shape His creation. If the creation does not develop into what the potter desires, he is free to reshape it. As Ruler of the universe, God can reshape His creation by overseeing its administration.

He rules in holiness and goodness. God sits on the throne of righteousness because He is holy. We never need to fear that He will act out of cruel motivation. He is a gracious sovereign who encourages us to "draw near with confidence to the throne of grace" (Hebrews 4:16). His holiness separates Him from His creation, allowing Him to divinely rule over creation. He oversees and controls history, hoping to reveal Himself and show His compassion to the world. We lead Christ's Church knowing that we may be piloting the ship, but it is God who is moving the ship forward. God is in control; we only communicate His vision and truths to His people.

God, the Compassionate Savior

The God revealed to us in Scripture is a God of compassion. He loves the Church He has created, and that same love should be its distinguishing characteristic. "Let us love one another, for love is from God; and everyone who loves is born of God and knows God. The one who does not love does not know God, for God is love. By this the love of God was manifested in us, that God has sent His only begotten Son into the world so that we might live through Him" (1 John 4:7–9). He calls us His followers—His children; and in the greatest act of love, He sent His own Son to die for our sins. God loves us and wants that same love to be a part of our lives. "A new commandment I give to you, that you love one another, even as I have loved you, that you also love one another" (John 13:34).

In His essential nature and in all of His actions, God loves. In a world that has distorted real love through hedonism and greed, we must turn to God to see real love. His love affects all the expressions of His character and attributes. The psalmist proclaims, "The LORD is good; His lovingkindness is everlasting" (Psalm 100:5). We were created as objects of God's love. Love becomes the doorway to knowing God in an intimate way. His love is unchanging and free. In fact, we can do nothing to prevent God from loving us, and we can do nothing to deserve His love. He is the source of all love.

Our view of God determines how we will relate to God. Our perception of God determines our entire life and ministry. It affects who we are and how we live every aspect of our lives. Our understanding of who God is and how we relate to Him determines our friends, our thoughts, our feelings, and our actions.

How big is our God? What does He look like? The Lord has given us a list of His many attributes. I (Bill) have chosen to highlight thirteen of God's attributes with our appropriate response to each of them.

63

Our Response to 13 Key Attributes of God

1. Because God is a personal Spirit, I will seek intimate fellowship with Him.

2. Because God is all-powerful, He can help me with anything.

3. Because God is ever-present, He is always with me.

4. Because God knows everything, I will go to Him with all my questions and concerns.

5. Because God is sovereign, I will joyfully submit to His will.

6. Because God is holy, I will devote myself to Him in purity, worship, and service.

7. Because God is absolute truth, I will believe what He says and live accordingly.

8. Because God is righteous, I will live by His standards.

9. Because God is just, He will always treat me fairly.

10. Because God is love, He is unconditionally committed to my well-being.

11. Because God is merciful, He forgives my sins when I sincerely confess them.

12. Because God is faithful, I will trust Him to always keep His promises.

13. Because God never changes, my future is secure and eternal.

Throughout the previous pages, we have attempted to talk about God. An adequate discussion would fill this book and a hundred more just like it. The longer we serve Him, the more we know of Him. He reveals Himself in new ways every day. We continue to learn more, and our picture of who God is grows and another color is added to the stained-glass window. Our prayer is that as leaders, we will continue to grow in the knowledge of our great God and Savior.

CONFIDENCE IN GOD'S WORD TO GUIDE US

God speaks to His people through His Word. Throughout this book, biblical stories are used not only as illustration but also as the basis for principles and strategy we must take to live beyond the limits. This is because the Bible is God's revelation of Himself to mankind, in which He reveals the plan of salvation. God's inspired, inerrant, holy Word serves as the roadmap, compass, clock, and guide on the journey of faith. Through God's Word, we receive an explanation of history, hope for the future, peace in the midst of trials, and direction when we are lost. When we obey His Word, we can trust in Him and confidently live the life of faith.

It is sad how many of God's people never consult the Word of God. Leaders must be "people of the Book," delighting in reading and studying the revelation of God. They must meditate on God's words. They have hidden the Bible in their hearts in order that they might not cause offense to God (Psalm 119:11). You cannot love someone whom you do not know, and you cannot know someone with whom you do not spend time. To know Him is to love Him. To love Him is to trust Him. To trust Him is to obey Him. To obey Him is to be blessed. To know Him, we must make the reading, studying, memorizing, and meditating on His Word a priority in our daily lives.

As we lead the church of tomorrow, we must be in God's Word today. This time with the Savior is the pivotal moment during the day where we connect with the Source of life and power. During these moments alone with God, He provides us with fuel for the day, and speaks and prepares us for the road we must travel together. It is important to remember that Daniel could face the lions with confidence because he talked with God daily.

Developing a quiet time with God can be one of the most rewarding and challenging parts of the Christian leader's walk. Many struggle with setting aside an hour or even thirty minutes a day with the Lord. There are many voices competing for the time of the Christian leader, and it is easy to become sidetracked and not allow this important aspect of the life of faith to be developed. It is possible to create a time to meet God alone. However, it is more than possible; it is necessary, for we cannot minister to others unless we have spent time with God. The following steps will help you to establish this time:

Prioritize the Word of God in Your Life

For many years, I (Bill) had no established time to study God's Word. At various times during the day, I would find moments alone with God. Several years ago, however, I was challenged to take Matthew 6:33 seriously: "Seek ye *first* the kingdom of God" (KJV, emphasis added). Since then, I have devoted my first waking moments each day to opening God's Word and immersing myself in the message God has for me. In Psalm 5:3, we learn that we are to seek the Lord in the morning. During this time, it has been my practice to read the entire Bible in a year.

We should have our quiet time in the morning because we are getting ready to live the day. Some may feel that they do not have half an hour to give for a time alone with God in the morning. Most people get up in a rush, read the paper, shower, have breakfast, and hurry out the door to work. It may be necessary to go to bed thirty minutes or an hour earlier in order to have more time in the morning. Set aside a time to study and meditate upon the Word of God. God is the source of power and life. Through the Word of God, we are transformed into leaders as we encounter God. As D. L. Moody has said, "The Bible will keep you from sin, or sin will keep you from the Bible."

Prepare for Your Time with the Lord

Do not approach your time with God haphazardly. Many leaders plan and prepare meetings with executives, deacons, or church staffs but never prepare for their meeting with God. Leaders don't just "wake up" and "meet God." They prepare themselves for the maximum benefit of receiving and communicating with God.

We must physically prepare for this time by being alert and undistracted. Determine what is the best time for you. Some people need to get dressed and have breakfast before beginning a quiet time. Others cannot become distracted by anything and immediately go to the Word of God. It may be necessary to accomplish light chores around the house because of family schedules and then meet with the Lord. The important thing is to be physically alert and ready to hear from God. I have sought to "seek God first" by reading and praying before I do anything else in the morning, including eating breakfast.

We must also be mentally alert. Our quiet time with God is not an extension of physical rest. Prayer and the study of God's Word are activities. We are to be active in the process of becoming mentally tough. This is work, not something we do when we are half-asleep or distracted. We must come expecting to receive a blessing from God.

Not only do we need to be alert, but we must also come before God morally pure. It is an insult to God when we ignore sin in our hearts or lives. A quiet time is fellowship with a holy God. Some people do not have a quiet time because they feel uncomfortable speaking to God due to their sin. If we harbor sin in our hearts, then God will not hear us when we pray (Psalm 66:18). We must first deal with our sin through confession and repentance before God will listen to anything we might want to say to Him.

We must plan the environment of our prayer time. Each morning Daniel opened the window toward Jerusalem and prayed to God. Jesus said, "When you pray, go into your inner room" (Matthew 6:6). Each of us needs a place where we can shut the door to the world and open the windows to heaven. We pray in private because we do not want anything to distract us from focusing on God. This place needs to be well-lit and well-ventilated. It becomes our special place of hope and trust in God. It is our tabernacle on earth where God meets us and we meet God. It is the secret place that is the sacred place. The mark of a good prayer life is not how we pray in public but how we pray in private.

We must prepare the tools of meditation. There are several practical items that will make our quiet time more effective. First, you should have a readable Bible, large enough for you to write in the margins and easy to read. When you wear out a Bible, save it and buy another one. A well-read Bible will become a best friend. A person who reads the Bible so frequently that it is falling apart probably has a life that is not. Your Bible will become a chronicle of your spiritual journey marked by ink and tears on the passages where God spoke to you.

Second, you need a loose-leaf devotional journal. In this journal, write down truths that you learned during your quiet time. Even if you think you have a good memory, the weakest ink is still better than the strongest memory. When reviewing the pages of the journal, it will be easy to see the pattern in which God is speaking to you. This is only possible if you record the intimate moments you have with the Master and view the entries collectively after the fact.

Third, a prayer journal is helpful to keep a list of those things for which you are praying. This will help to make sure you are praying about the things that are on your heart. A good prayer journal will keep you focused on your prayer needs on any given morning. In this journal, make a list of people and the needs you pray for each day. Ask God to help you to prioritize the list. Even while you are praying, there will be other people or things that come to your mind. Write them down and keep seeking the Lord on their behalf.

Study the Whole Word of God

How big is your Bible? If God removed all the books of the Bible you do not read, what size would the remaining portion of your Bible be? The first activity of your prayer life should be to read and the study the Scriptures. Every minister needs to develop a systematic way to read and study God's Word in depth each year. The Bible is the holy, inspired, inerrant Word that is filled with power. If the Bible is not a vital part of your daily living and you are not feasting on the Word of God daily, you will never be a strong Christian. We encourage you to memorize Colossians 3:16,17:

> Remember what Christ taught and let his words enrich your lives and make you wise; teach them to each other and sing them out in psalms and hymns and spiritual songs, singing to the Lord with thankful hearts. And whatever you do or say, let it be as a representative of the Lord Jesus and come with him into the presence of God the Father to give him your thanks (TLB).

For study of God's Word, it is important to read manageable portions of Scripture daily. Reading a hundred psalms each day or only a short passage such as one or two verses rarely allows the full impact of the Scriptures to mold our lives. Many resources are available to categorize and assist the leader in studying God's Word. We suggest that a leader plan to read the Bible through each year. Organize your study by utilizing the divisions of paragraphs and chapters. Read the portion of Scripture more than once. Study the passage; do not merely glance at it.

During this study, it is often during the third or fourth time of reading through a passage that God gives special insights in the text. Read the Word first and pray second. God already knows everything about us, but we do not know everything about God. It is more important for you to hear from God than God to hear from you at this point. Read the Word carefully and systematically. Read from the Psalms for worship and Proverbs for wisdom.

When you read the Bible, use common sense. Do not jump all over the text with no thought or plan. Have a balance in your reading. Devotional books are wonderful, but this is not the place for devotional books; this is the time for the inspired words of God to become incarnate in your life.

Meditate on the Word of God

After reading God's Word, stop and meditate on the words. Think through the concepts and truths presented. Apply them to your life. Do not be content with a casual reading of God's Word but mine the text for nuggets of truth and application. Pray the passage aloud and ask God to reveal Himself to you through the text. Many texts of the Bible are complex and require considerable meditation to "work through" in the human mind. This is not problematic but necessary for the Christian walk of faith. God wants us to trust Him and depend upon Him to speak to our hearts and our minds.

In *Manna in the Morning*, Stephen Olford suggests that we approach the text by asking the following questions:

1. Is there a command to obey?

2. Is there a promise to claim?

3. Is there a sin to forsake?

4. Is there a lesson to learn?

5. Is there a new truth to take with me?[2]

Walk through each of these questions in your heart and in your mind. Think through each question carefully. As you meditate, the answers will come from God and His Word. In your prayer journal, record what God speaks to you about the passage of Scripture. This is not for others but for your own spiritual development. Make it personal. These moments with God and His Word are not the time for leaders to develop their sermon material. It is true that many of our messages and thoughts develop out of our personal time with God, but this is not the purpose of meeting each morning. During these quiet times, God may speak individually to the leader, addressing areas that are private and specific to the life of the believer. Often, the words revealed during the quiet time are not intended to be shared with anyone else.

Obey What God Has Told You

The visions and dreams given to us must be lived out. When God leads us to seek forgiveness of others, we must search out those persons and repent before them. Our spiritual train runs on two separate rails. One rail is insight, and the other is instruction. These rails make up revelation and obedience. If our lives get off the track, we will cease to have power with God.

Through His Word, God builds direction and faith in us. It is through His holy, inspired Word that we draw closer to Him. The church of the future is rooted in the Bible. While many are disregarding it in the postmodern world, it is the commitment to God's Word that will separate the synergistic church from others and move it beyond the limits of relativism and power-lessness. A church that is not committed to the Bible will be grasping for truth in the days ahead. As moral relativism and religious pluralism invade the world, only those who have confidence in the Word of God will be able to live the life of faith.

CONFIDENCE IN THE HOLY SPIRIT TO EMPOWER US

Jesus sent the Holy Spirit to comfort, convict, and empower the believer to be a fruitful witness for Him (John 16; Acts 1). The Holy Spirit is the particular person of the Trinity through whom the entire triune Godhead works in us.[3] The Holy Spirit is God. He is an active member of the Trinity. People frequently react to distorted views and wrong interpretations of God's Spirit by saying things like, "We don't want the Holy Spirit," or "The Holy Spirit is not for me." To say we do not want the Holy Spirit active in our lives is to say we do not want God in our lives. We see in God's Word that references to the Holy Spirit are interchangeable with references to God. In Acts 5, Peter confronts Ananias and Sapphira for lying to the Holy Spirit (v. 3). In the next verse he asserts, "You have not lied to men but to God." It is clear from verse 4 that Peter understood the Holy Spirit and God to be equal. We strongly affirm that the Holy Spirit is literally indispensable since no act of our Christian faith—birth, life, worship, fellowship, service, or mission—would be possible without Him.[4]

The Holy Spirit is a person; He is not an "it" or a "thing." He is not an impersonal force as in New Age religions. In John 16:13,14, the Bible uses the masculine pronoun when speaking of the Holy Spirit. The Holy Spirit engages in actions that are performed by people: He thinks, feels, teaches, speaks, commands, testifies, and reveals. The Holy Spirit is God just as fully and in the same way as are the Father and the Son.[6] In light of these truths, we should treat the Spirit as a person and regard Him as the infinite loving God within our heart, worthy of our worship.

In addition to the person and work of the Holy Spirit, it is important to understand that God gave the Spirit as a gift to His people. We must receive this gift and allow Him to operate in our lives to accomplish what God has called us to do. In John 16:7, Jesus said, "I will send Him to you." Jesus states plainly that the Spirit's presence would be more advantageous than His own personal presence on the earth—meaning that when Jesus left His disciples, He would send them the Holy Spirit who would help them to grow more in Christ. This was the fulfillment of many Old Testament prophecies. Ezekiel recorded that God said, "I will put My Spirit within you and cause you to walk in My statutes, and you will be careful to observe My ordinances" (36:27). Joel spoke of a last-day outpouring of God's Spirit upon all flesh (2:28–32). Jesus' last instructions to His disciples were to wait in Jerusalem to receive the gift of the Holy Spirit (Acts 1:4,5).

The Power of the Holy Spirit

Jesus told His disciples, "You will receive power when the Holy Spirit has come upon you; and you shall be My witnesses both in Jerusalem, and in all Judea and Samaria, and even to the remotest part of the earth" (Acts 1:8). The nature of the power is evident. It is the coming of God to man for the accomplishment of a divine purpose in this sacred partnership. The natural result of the infilling of the Holy Spirit is power—power to serve and to communicate effectively as leaders. Without the power of the Holy Spirit, leaders are unable to exert the effort, meet the responsibilities, and fulfill the ministry required of them. The Spirit of God turned the disciples from scared followers who denied their Master into sacred proclaimers of the gospel of Jesus Christ. When he was filled with the Spirit, Peter could stand before the multitude and proclaim the good news of Jesus Christ—the same Peter who had denied he knew Christ three times the night Jesus was betrayed.

Dwight L. Moody was an average young man. But at the age of 17, he made a commitment to Christ in the back room of the shoe store where he worked. His life was changed. He began inviting everyone he could to his church. When he attempted to preach, one of the deacons assured him that he could serve God best by keeping silent. Another member praised the young man for his zeal, but recommended that he realize his limitations and not attempt to speak in public.

> "It lies within the man himself whether he will or will not make that entire and full consecration."

Moody went on to preach to millions and to be used by God to draw thousands upon thousands into Christ's kingdom.

What made the difference in the life of this ordinary man? At the beginning of Moody's ministry, he accepted the challenge of a Mr. Henry Varley: "The world has yet to see what God will do with and for and through and in and by the man who is fully consecrated to Him." As Moody reflected on these wise words, he thought, "He said 'a man.' He did not say a great man, nor a learned man, nor a smart man, but simply 'a man.' I am a man and it lies within the man himself whether he will or will not make that entire and full consecration."[7]

That day D. L. Moody gave all of himself to his Savior and Lord. He invited Christ to live in and through him—and that made all the difference.

Our victory in Christ, like the victory D. L. Moody experienced, is possible only by living in Christ's power. Are you ready for your messages to be transformed? Are you ready to see hundreds, even thousands, introduced to Jesus Christ through your ministry? Are you ready to experience God in ways you have never felt before? If you want these benefits in your life and ministry, you want to be filled with the Spirit.

Paul's prayer in Ephesians 3:14–21 asks God to strengthen the Ephesians with power through the Spirit so that Christ could live in their hearts and they might better know and understand the love of God. When Paul came to Corinth and preached Jesus Christ, he did not come on his own. In 1 Corinthians 2:4,5, we read that when Paul preached, his sermons were accompanied by a demonstration of the Spirit's power. This was so that the faith of the Corinthians would not rest upon man but upon God. Jesus did not send His disciples into the world until they had first received the Holy Spirit on the Day of Pentecost. The result of that filling of the Spirit was a mighty harvest of souls for God's kingdom. When the apostles were confronted with adversity in Acts 4:29–31, they prayed that the Spirit would give them boldness to proclaim the message of truth. God answered their prayer, and the place where they were praying was shaken. The Holy Spirit's power will affect everything it comes in contact with, even the natural world.

The Need for the Holy Spirit's Power

We cannot live an abundant, effective, fruitful Christian life without the power of the Holy Spirit. Even Jesus Christ lived a Spirit-filled life. The Holy Spirit was present in every aspect of His life and ministry. The Holy Spirit caused Mary to conceive and give birth to Christ, thereby making His life on earth possible. The Holy Spirit descended upon Christ at His baptism and then led Him into the wilderness to be tempted by Satan. In a synagogue in Nazareth, Jesus began His ministry by declaring, with a quote from Isaiah, "The Spirit of the Lord is upon Me, because He anointed Me to preach the gospel to the poor. He has sent Me to proclaim release to the captives, and recovery of sight to the blind, to set free those who are oppressed, to proclaim the favorable year of the Lord" (Luke 4:18,19). The Holy Spirit worked through Christ as He ministered in first-century Palestine.

Ministers must also be filled with the Holy Spirit for their ministry. If the Spirit of God fell upon Jesus to enable Him to preach the good news, how much more do we need the Spirit of God to lead us and guide us? The Spirit is the enabler, the empowerer, the equipper, the counselor, and the helper. The Holy Spirit bears witness of Christ and reminds us of Christ's teaching (John 14:26). The Holy Spirit indwells and empowers every believer (1 Corinthians 6:19). It is the Holy Spirit who manifests Christ's nature within us; if we don't have the Spirit, we don't have Christ (Romans 8:9).

What an amazing privilege to have the same Holy Spirit who empowered our Savior living inside us! Only through the presence of the Holy Spirit can we experience a supernatural life because the Holy Spirit works in us to reflect Christ in our lives. From the moment we are born spiritually, He gives each believer the power to live a supernatural life and be fruitful for Him. The Bible assures us, "His divine power has given us everything we need for life and godliness through our knowledge of Him who called us by His own glory and goodness" (2 Peter 1:3, NIV). Despite God's gracious provision, we may suffer power shortages and brownouts in our lives. We may fail to understand the power available to us. We may short-circuit the flow of that power in our lives by sin, unbelief, or a failure to spend time with God, the source of all spiritual power.

Why do we need this power? In *Living Supernaturally in Christ*, I (Bill) detail five reasons all believers need God's power in their lives. The leaders of the synergistic church are even more dependent upon God's power because they must guide God's people. These reasons form the acrostic POWER:

P – Proclaim the gospel boldly

O – Overcome evil forces in the world and spiritual realm
W – Withstand personal temptation and adversity
E – Embrace God's perfect will for your life
R – Reflect God's character (Galatians 5:23)[8]

Becoming a Vessel of God's Power

It is imperative that every pastor, evangelist, and missionary become a vessel of God's power. Every minister of the gospel, indeed every believer, is made "a servant of this gospel by the gift of God's grace given [us] through the working of his power" (Ephesians 3:7, NIV). It has been said, "God means business with those who mean business with Him." Make it your highest aim to live and serve God and your people in the mighty power of the Holy Spirit, drawing upon the supernatural resources of the triune God.

There are moments when a single act says more than an encyclopedia could. Sometimes an entire life can be summarized by one significant action. The story of Elijah and Elisha demonstrates one of those scriptural events that say more than words ever could. It was when God's servant, Elijah, cast his mantle upon his successor, Elisha. The mantle was Elijah's divine logo or his identifying mark. It was a dramatic time when Elijah left Mount Sinai and traveled 150 miles north to Damascus in obedience to the voice of God. On his journey, God directed him to a young man plowing in the field. He veered off the road and, without a word, took his prophet's mantle and threw it upon the young man and continued down the road. The biblical account of Elijah and Elisha illustrates several junctures on this journey that leaders need to traverse in order to impact their generation.

Leaders Have a Priority to Practice (1 Kings 19:19–21)

When God calls us, He brings us to a point of decision. After Elijah had been renewed and revived in the cave, the voice of God told him to return to a difficult place. God told him to go back to where Ahab had a price on his head, back to the place where Jezebel wanted his life, back to the place where Baal worship still influenced an entire nation. It would have been easy to stay in the cave on Mount Horeb where there was an earthquake, wind, fire, and the voice of God, yet God called him to go back to a place of difficulty. Elijah still had seven or eight years of dynamic ministry left.

When Elijah placed his mantle upon Elisha, it was clear he was saying, "Follow me." We have been called to a Man, not a movement; to a Person, not a plan; to Christ, not a church. Jesus said, "Follow Me, and I will make you fishers of men." The Bible tells us that they immediately left their nets and followed Him (Matthew 4:19,20, NIV). Elisha left his family and his yoke of oxen, and the disciples left their families and their fishing to follow Jesus. Have you prioritized your life? Are you truly willing to become what Christ has commanded you to be as a person and as a leader?

At the end of 1 Kings 19:21, we see that Elisha began to follow Elijah and minister to him. We all must learn to minister *to* Christ before we can minister *for* Christ. We are to become servants of Jesus Christ. It is the Holy Spirit who teaches us to live in humility serving Christ. In 2 Kings 3:11, we are told that Elisha poured water on the hands of Elijah. This passage indicates that Elisha took the place of a slave to serve Elijah. He ministered to his master. Is it your purpose and burning ambition to serve Jesus Christ? When you are treated like a servant, you will know whether or not you are a servant. Dr. Steve Douglass served at my side (Bill) for over thirty years before God chose Him to follow me as president of Campus Crusade for Christ.

After Elisha accepted the call to become Elijah's disciple, his name is not mentioned for another seven to eight years. During these years, he served God in the shadow of Elijah as a disciple. However, after those eight years of study, he spent sixty-five years in dynamic ministry for God. The Spirit of God often develops us in the shadows. We are prepared before our work is needed. It may take years of the Holy Spirit's work to develop us into the leaders we need to be. We must be willing to take the long view, not the short view, understanding that the time in the shadows is not wasted time. We need to be ready when the time comes to supernaturally lead others and impact our world for Christ.

On the afternoon of June 2, 1925, the New York Yankees were preparing for a game against the Washington Senators. The veteran first baseman, Walley Pips, said to his manager, Miller Huggins, "I have a headache. I don't want to play." Huggins turned to a young man named Lou Gehrig and said, "Lou, you play first base." Lou Gehrig, a nobody, stepped out of the shadows and played 2,130 consecutive games, a record that stood for almost seventy years. One man stepped aside and another stepped into the spotlight. If Gehrig had not been preparing before the opportunity came his way, he would not have been ready and the chance would have passed him by. Leaders are not developed overnight. They prepare themselves daily for what Christ desires for them to be and do in their generation. You may be frustrated that you are living in the "shadow times." You have big dreams and grand plans, but your life seems not to be going fast enough. Do not let your ego or impatience limit what God can do for you. Live beyond the limits of your own pride and have faith in God.

> The Spirit of God often develops us in the shadows. We are prepared before our work is needed.

Leaders Have a Price to Pay (1 Kings 19:19–21)

Leading Christ's church will cost us something. Life is made up of tradeoffs. We cannot do everything. The leader who desires to live in the power of God's Spirit must be willing to abandon the things of this world. In Elijah's period of history, individuals who owned oxen were considered wealthy. Elisha had several servants and twelve oxen. It is obvious he came from an affluent family. God found Elisha working in the fields—in the midst of the ordinary, not the extraordinary. God does not usually call us in the red-hot heat of the dramatic. We do not live our lives in the sensational or the unpredictable. God's call usually comes while we are in the office, the home, the car, or our prayer closet. Then suddenly, the ordinary becomes the extraordinary; the natural becomes the supernatural. Elisha left his position to become a slave and servant to Elijah. Elisha gave up his *professional responsibilities* to follow his master.

Elisha was also willing to surrender his *private relationships*. When Elijah laid his mantle upon Elisha, Elisha ran to Elijah and asked if he could go back and kiss his parents good-bye. Elijah gave a concealed answer: "Go back again, for what have I done to you?" (v. 20). Did Elijah condemn or commend him? Elijah did not condemn him. He knew that this was a moment of decision. Elijah knew that God, not he, was calling Elisha to a life of discipleship. He simply laid the mantle upon him because God told him to do so. There are to be no earthly relationships that come ahead of our affection for Christ.

A life of service to God comes with a price. Elisha killed the oxen and sacrificed them on the wood of the plow he had been using in the field. He invited his family and friends and dramatically announced that he was burning his bridges behind him and becoming a disciple of Elijah. Is there anything you own that you would not give up to follow Jesus Christ? A business? A dream? A possession?

A disciple says there is no price too high to pay to be a follower of Jesus Christ. Elisha, who would have inherited his father's estate, was willing to sacrifice his *personal riches*. Are we willing to forsake all that God's power might be seen at work in our life and ministry?

Leaders Have a Perspective to Perceive (2 Kings 2:1–8)

We read in 2 Kings 2 that Elijah was taken to heaven in a whirlwind. There are only two ascension stories in the Bible—one in the Old Testament (Elijah) and one in the New Testament (Jesus). While Enoch walked with God and God took him to heaven, Elijah and Jesus are the only two who ascended into heaven in front of people. Only the personal disciples of the two who ascended witnessed these ascensions. Supernatural power is often most profoundly seen in private, not in the public arena. The empowerment of the Spirit is most often conferred in the prayer closet.

Some are trapped in the philosophy that bigger is better. They have fallen victim to a worldly view of power. They look for opportunities to showcase their leadership abilities and talents. They confuse spectacle with Spirit, announcement with anointing, publicity with power, and big with blessing. They limit the work of the Spirit because they are looking for an event rather than the Spirit's process. Synergistic leaders rely upon God's power to work in their churches and in other people's lives, not upon their own charisma.

If we are to be disciples of Jesus Christ, there are many things that can cause us not to stay focused. These are tests to see if disciples are resolute in their purpose. Elijah tested Elisha. He told him to stay while he traveled on, but Elisha would not be deterred. He pursued Elijah. Are you easily deterred from following Christ? Does it take very much to get you off-track in your relationship with God? There are obstacles to becoming a disciple of Christ. Elijah was testing Elisha's determination to be a disciple. Many times we are easily persuaded not to follow the Lord. God saves the best for those who are faithful to the end. Elijah was showing Elisha how to be prepared at all times to meet God. He led his fellow servants from Gilgal on to Bethel, then to Jericho and finally to Jordan. In other words, if we are going to be ready to meet the Lord, we have to be willing to move from the place of beginning (Gilgal), to the place of breaking (Bethel), to the place of battles (Jericho), in order to reach the place of beholdings (Jordan). It is the Holy Spirit who enables us to pursue the vision God has given us. We must be careful not to be sidetracked by imitations.

Leaders Have a Power to Possess
(2 Kings 2:9–15)

We must possess the power that has been given to us. In his final moments, Elijah asked Elisha what he could do for him. Elisha said he wanted a double portion of the spirit of Elijah to be upon him. He had seen God's power working in Elijah, and he wanted that same experience. When we become a true Galatians 2:20 kind of disciple, our Master is able to work powerfully in and through us.

When Elijah ascended in a whirlwind of fire, his mantle of power fell to the earth. Elisha bent over and put it on his shoulders. Because God had chosen Elisha to serve Him, God equipped him with all the power necessary to fulfill his tasks. Jesus promised His disciples the same power for service. Jesus said, "I am going to send you what my Father has promised; but stay in the city until you have been clothed with power from on high." Then, while He was blessing them, He left them and was taken up into heaven (Luke 24:49–51, NIV).

In Acts 2:4, the promised Spirit fell upon Jesus' disciples. Peter tells us that the gift is for all of us today. To be the leaders

Christ has called us to be, we must humble ourselves to allow the Holy Spirit to work through us. Elisha's power was linked to the ascension of Elijah. Our power is linked to the ascension of Jesus. When Jesus ascended, He sent the Comforter to abide in us. When Jesus went up, the Holy Spirit came down, the disciples went out, and the lost came in. When the mantle came down, Elisha had to appropriate it—he submitted his life to God's will. Have we received the power that is potentially ours? The first time the mantle was placed on Elisha's shoulders by someone else; however, the second time, he had to put on the mantle himself. Though we are given the Holy Spirit when we are born again, we must choose to die daily to allow Him to have preeminence in our lives. If you get the full picture, you will see that just as God continued His work through Elisha, Christ lives His life in us and continues His work through us, His servants. Christianity is not what we do for Christ but what He accomplishes in and through us.

When Elisha took that mantle and went to the Jordan River, he struck the water and asked, "Where is the LORD, the God of Elijah?" (v. 14). The power that had been on Elijah was now with Elisha. Some have the idea that the best days of the Church are in the past, but we are confident that the best days are ahead of us. The kingdom of God is not about to stop. We have confidence in God that He will continue to build the Church in the twenty-first century because we know that we have the power of the Spirit working within us to accomplish that task. Nations have died for lack of leadership; corporations have folded because there were no successors to keep them going; institutions have withered after decades of prosperity because of a lack of new leadership. Yet, after 2,000 years, the Church has moved from generation to generation with God raising up men and women called to supernaturally lead God's people. We do not have to worry about the Church. Jesus Christ will continue to raise up dynamic leadership until the end of the age. If we will only love and obey Him, He will empower each generation to help fulfill the Great Commission and build His Church.

In 1889, D. L. Moody asked Rubin A. Torrey to help him with his evangelistic work. Moody made Torrey the president of Moody Bible Institute in Chicago, Illinois. When Moody experienced a heart attack in Kansas City in 1899, Torrey took over the campaign and finished it successfully. Torrey influenced a young man named J. Wilbur Chapman. Charles M. Alexander, Torrey's minister of music, joined Chapman in a worldwide evangelism tour from 1909 to 1914. When Chapman finished his tour, he found a young man named Billy Sunday in Chicago. Billy Sunday became Chapman's associate. A year later, Billy Sunday was holding his own evangelistic meetings. He was an energetic baseball player who became an evangelist. Billy Sunday later influenced an evangelist named Mordecai Ham. In 1901, Ham began fifty years of itinerant evangelism. On the last night of a four-week crusade when he was in Charlotte, North Carolina, a clothing merchant named J. D. Prevette went to the back row where two young men were sitting. One boy was named Wilson and the other Graham. Prevette witnessed to Grady Wilson and Billy Graham about Christ that evening. Wilson and Graham came forward and gave their lives to Christ. A line can be drawn from the ministry of D. L. Moody of the 1860s to the present Billy Graham. Each of these men experienced the Holy Spirit's power. They practiced the right priorities, paid the price, perceived the right perspective, and possessed the power of the Holy Spirit.

CHAPTER 4

Called by God

It is amazing how many people, even in ministry, struggle with lack of fulfillment and doubts concerning their calling. They face seemingly insurmountable challenges and wonder whether they are truly fulfilling their calling in life. They desire a sense of mission, a direction and goal, so that when they have accomplished it, they can feel that they have truly heard and followed the voice of God.

If this sense of purpose and mission is not identified, they will struggle throughout their entire ministry. Until those in leadership know they are called by the Father to do His will, they will be filled with uncertainty and disappointment. On the other hand, those who follow the voice of God and finish the task set before them live a meaningful life. As Bob Buford said, their lives are not just a success; their lives are significant.[1] The calling of God provides direction and guidance for life and ministry. It gives a sense of "divine destiny."

THE TWOFOLD CALLING

Do you know what your mission is in life? How can you know

if you are making progress unless you have a purpose? Do you worry that your life and ministry are meaningless? Whether you are just beginning in ministry or have been in leadership for some time, you must consider the following question: Why do you do what you do in the ministry? Is it simply to have a full calendar, money in the bank, or a local or national platform? Do you preach without purpose and minister without mission? We must never forget that Jesus Christ could speak His mission in one clear, concise sentence: "I came that they might have life, and might have it abundantly" (John 10:10). This mission was passed on to His disciples. They knew what their purpose in life was for they had been sent out to point others to new life in Christ (Romans 6:23). Before Christ ascended into heaven, He gave them the Great Commission. Their goal was world evangelization and the creation of disciples for Jesus Christ.

We are each called to fulfill that same commission; but we also must realize that within the universal calling of God, there is a unique and special calling for each of us. Peter was called to preach on the Day of Pentecost and to lead the church in Rome. James was to help the Jerusalem church through an early crisis. John was to record the great revelation of the end times and write letters of encouragement to the church. Each fulfilled the divine call upon their lives. They obeyed the Great Commission, but they also lived their own specific God-given mission.

Leaders must listen to the voice of God to know what He would have them do, and must submit to His direction. Many assume there is only one calling and that is to "go into all the world and preach the gospel" (Mark 16:15). While it is the calling of every believer to fulfill the Great Commission and evangelize the lost, He has chosen some to serve in full-time ministry. This calling is not distinct from the Great Commission; it is congruent with it. The general call to evangelize is complementary to the specific call upon an individual life. They are part and parcel of the same direction from God.

Our prayer has been that the Holy Spirit would raise up unique, dynamic, evangelistic leaders all over the world. Every snowflake is different and powerless on its own; yet when they get together, they can stop traffic as well as create beautiful scenery. Just like the snowflake, each of us has a unique mission and ministry—we look different from each other. However, when we work together, we can blanket the world with the gospel. This is the reason God gives us each individual callings. None of us is called to be just like another person. We have been given a mission that when united with others makes a powerful impact.

The calling of God is more than a mission/vision statement. It is more than a written set of core values and five-year goals, although each of these can be a reflection of God's calling. Our purpose is not to teach you how to write a mission statement or set goals for ministry, although we suggest you write out your goals and mission in life. However, you cannot write your mission until you have heard the voice of God clearly calling you. We will not attempt to delineate the specifics of your own individual calling. Even if we could, we would not do it. The calling of God is so specific and so holy that it can be birthed and nurtured only through the inspiration of the divine. It can come only from God to you as you seek after Him; it cannot be created or derived from a formula. In each of our lives, our mission is born from above while our vision is lived on earth. The leader's life is the expression of his God-inspired calling. We will, however, seek to help you understand the nature of God's calling and the way we should live in light of that calling.

Synergy is working together with others. It is the total collaboration of all parties involved in an adventure. The adventure of ministry is wrapped completely in the calling of God. If you are doing things you are not called by God to do, then you need to stop them immediately. Pursue God and pursue His calling upon your life. We challenge you to seek God's will through fasting and prayer.

THE NATURE OF GOD'S CALLING

God communicates and ordains the calling on an individual's life. Paul's calling began before the creation of the world (Galatians 1:15). God knew Jeremiah before he was formed in his mother's womb (Jeremiah 1:5). Leaders who desire long-term effective ministry must know without a doubt that God has called them into ministry. This leads to a sense of providence in our lives and ministry. The word "providence" is derived from the Latin *providentia*, which principally means "foresight or foreknowledge." When God calls a person into full-time ministry, He has foreknowledge of how this individual can make a unique contribution to the fulfillment of the Great Commission.

While the doctrine of providence means God's supernatural ability to see ahead of time, it also includes God's ability to *govern* all creatures, actions, and things according to His immutable counsel, without violating man's free will. This is good news for Christian workers. God not only sees the potential we have for Him in ministry, but also is at work using circumstances, both good and bad, to achieve His master-plan for our lives and ministries.

When problems arise, the Holy Trinity does not meet in an emergency session and say, "We did not see that problem coming. That one caught us by surprise." God sees everything ahead of time. Long before Adam and Eve fell in the Garden of Eden, God, in His mind, had already placed a cross on Calvary. Before you were placed in your leadership position, God already was working to help you during this time. Those who have been called into full-time ministry have providence attached to their lives. Understanding the importance of their calling will help them to better hear from God and allow the Holy Spirit to illuminate their mission in life.

Without the assurance of this call, we will find the ministry we pursue difficult or impossible. Just as Christians in general need to have assurance of their salvation and must move forward in their Christian walk by faith, so ministers in particular need to know they have been called into full-time ministry and, by faith, move forward in their service to Christ and their community. Ministers who question their calling to preach the gospel normally question almost everything else they do in the ministry. They become unsure of themselves and do not aggressively pursue ministry.

Life and ministry are filled with change. Nothing remains constant, even in ministry. Having an unchanging sense of who we are, what we are about, and what we value is the key to having the ability to change.[2] When the surroundings change and the strong winds blow, the divine providential calling is the anchor that will hold us. It is this calling that keeps us going despite the changing wind. It is knowing that God has providentially called us for such a time as this (Esther 4:14).

GOD PROVIDENTIALLY CALLS LEADERS

Although our calling in life is sacred and holy, most people have never spent time identifying their unique calling. It is amazing that most people spend more time planning for a two-week vacation than they spend planning for the rest of their lives. Our calling must be pursued through prayer and will develop inside of us over a period of time. It is not only through impressions or a sudden realization that God speaks to us. The call and mission of leaders are based on a lifetime of God's speaking and guiding them.

God does not want your calling to be perplexing. There are many sincere Christians who want to do the will of God but do not know how to go about discovering His will for their lives. By applying the "sound mind principle," we can better understand what God's will is for our lives.

The "sound mind principle" is based on 2 Timothy 1:7: "God hath not given us the spirit of fear; but of power, and of love, and of a sound mind" (KJV). This mind is being renewed and is under the control of the Holy Spirit when we offer ourselves to God as His servants (Romans 12:1,2). Christians who yield their lives fully to Christ can be assured of sanctified reason and a sound mind. Therefore, we can use wisdom and guidance to determine God's will for our lives. So many people are looking for a divine, cataclysmic event that they miss the plan God has laid out clearly for them. While all callings are unique, the call to leadership has characteristics that are universal.

The Characteristics of a Divine Calling

When God calls us to His service, the calling is purposeful. God calls leaders to accomplish specific tasks. Moses was called to lead the Israelites out of Egyptian bondage. Joshua was called to lead Israel in the conquest of Canaan. The Old Testament prophets were called to proclaim the word of the Lord for their times. Paul was called to preach the gospel to the Gentiles. What is God calling you to do? What unique purpose do you fulfill in the kingdom of God? If you are an evangelist, why should a pastor invite you for a crusade instead of another evangelist? If you are serving as a pastor, what contribution can you bring to your community or city that other pastors cannot bring to your area? What is your local church known for? What distinguishes it from others? Is that distinguishing trait positive or negative? How does it relate to your calling?

Each member plays a vital part in the kingdom of God. Each of us is divinely gifted and placed in the Body of Christ to achieve a purpose. Defining our roles and goals in life will help us to find and fulfill our purpose. Roles provide direction, and goals determine the destination toward which we are heading. Leaders understand that a vision becomes a goal when they place a date by it. A date gives a sense of chronology and progression in one's life and mission.

The calling of God is very personal. God's hand was upon each of our lives long before we took our first steps as children. If we have been divinely called into a full-time preaching ministry, then God personally set us apart to preach the gospel. Preaching is much easier when preachers know that the providential hand of God has been laid upon their lives. Each of us has our own individual race to run. It would be tragic for our lives to come to a close and our personal race still not be completed. In his book for business leaders, *Business as a Calling*, Michael Novak gives us insight on individual callings:

> Each of us is as unique in our calling as we are in being made in the image of God. (It would take an infinite number of human beings, St. Thomas Aquinas once wrote, to mirror back the infixed facets of the Godhead. Each person reflects on a small—but beautiful—part of the whole.)[3]

Our calling is a reflection of God in us and in our ministries, and is one more representation of God's beauty in the world. The call is not just a job or vocation but also a divine act of God. Each of our callings is a different expression of God. As we are each made in the image of God and are being formed more each day into the image of His Son, we are fulfilling God's call upon our lives.

The calling of God is also practical. The calling God places on our lives will match our God-given abilities and gifts. One of the reasons many people do not recognize their gifts is because they seem natural.[4] While the typical pattern in Scripture is that God calls and equips the least likely individual to accomplish His will, He can use our natural gifts and talents as well.

What is it that we "naturally" do well? Many times the calling of God on our lives is very evident from what we seemingly do well naturally. It is our responsibility to recognize these gifts and use them in our service for God. Those who are natural organizers and administrators most likely are called to serve God in an administrative capacity. Those who naturally write well should utilize that "natural" or God-given talent to fulfill their calling. God's calling on our life is practical. When lived out, it makes perfect sense in the life God has given us. God planned our calling before we were created, and He orchestrates the experiences of our lives and the talents that reside within us to achieve this calling.

Finally, the calling of God is powerful. The study of Scripture reveals that God-called servants are endowed with a special anointing to fulfill the task to which He has called them. A defined call provides both the passion for the necessary creativity and the renewed energy for the daily grind. Novak writes

> Facing hard tasks necessarily exacts dread. Indeed, there are times when we wish we did not have to face every burden our calling imposes on us. Still, finding ourselves where we are and with the responsibilities we bear, we know it is our duty—part of what we're meant to do—to soldier on...There is an odd satisfaction in bearing certain pains.[5]

The calling God places on our lives may not be easy. It may be filled with distractions and hardships, but the calling provides the energy and power to persevere. God's calling in our lives is something that will excite us. Enthusiasm comes from the root words *en* and *theos*, which literally mean "in God."[6] What are we enthusiastic or "in God" about? The calling of God for leadership is a calling that empowers.

The Uniqueness of the Divine Call

Just knowing and understanding the nature and characteristics of God's calling are helpful in identifying and fulfilling that calling. However, each of us must determine whether success or significance is motivating the ministry we do. Success is timely and ends when we die. Significance is timeless and lives on after we die. The issue is not whether we are going to die or live forever. The latest statistics regarding death are pretty consistent. There are good odds that one day each of us is going to breathe our last breath and instantly be in the presence of God. When this happens, will we have lived a significant life? Will we have fulfilled the calling of God in our life? There are many successful people who never live significant lives because they have accomplished tasks, not fulfilled their calling. It must be the prayer of every leader to become who he is in Christ and to become the living fulfillment of the calling God has placed on his life.

People frequently ask: "What is the secret to your success?" "What quality or characteristic can I incorporate into my life to make me a successful minister?" "What can I do that is new and invigorating that will help me become the minister God wants me to be?" Those who ask these questions are often well-intentioned men and women wanting to begin a powerful, fruitful ministry. Sometimes they are not seeing the results they anticipated when they first began the work of the ministry. They have been to every church growth conference, some of them twice or more. Their libraries are filled with the latest books and manuals on how to *do* church and how to *do* a relationship with Jesus, yet nothing is working. Their ministry and their walk with God are floundering in an ocean of turmoil and disappointments.

> In Christ's work, there are no short-cuts and God does not make copies— only originals.

While their questions are motivated by good intentions, people make the mistake of trying to copy what others are doing, looking for shortcuts to fruitful ministry. In Christ's work, there are no shortcuts and God does not make copies—He only makes originals. It is impossible to replicate the ministry of others. Leaders must seek to learn and apply principles and ministry techniques from others, not simply listen and copy.

When we are approached with questions and we sense a real hunger for more of God and a more effective ministry, we will ask some probing questions. It is amazing that so few of the principles presented here are active in the lives of those asking the questions. They are so busy looking for the new and catchy that they forget to exercise the basic components of Christian faith and ministry to find the answers! We ask them, "When did you last discipline yourself through prayer and fasting?" It is not the new things that are hard to do, but the basic elements of the Christian walk with which they struggle. Simple things like prayer and Scripture memorization are often neglected. These leaders want to copy the methods of others without trying to become more like Jesus Christ themselves. The keys to leadership are not being used to unlock the difficult leadership positions in which they find themselves.

Sadly, many people can't seem to see providentially or realistically what God is calling them to do. It is only through His work in our lives and His calling that we fully realize our potential. We must become who God intended us to be. When we ignore the calling of God on our lives, we never fully become all God has called us to be. Instead, we settle for an incomplete picture of the life God has called us to live. We need to become who we are in Christ and not who we think we need to be. Our true identity or self-worth is much greater than any level of ministry we may have. In a sense, our uniqueness dies when we choose not to mature in our ministries. Everyone is young once, but we can be immature the rest of our lives if we so choose.

IMITATION—THE DEATH OF SELF

God has not called us to fulfill someone else's mission and ministry. Many ministers do not experience the life God wants for them because they are trying to copy others. But when we seek merely to copy others, we cease to be ourselves. God does not call an evangelist or a pastor to develop a ministry on the proven personality of someone else but on proven eternal principles. There is already one Billy Graham, Rick Warren, John Maxwell, and Bill Hybels in the world; God does not need another. We must be ourselves in ministry.

Whether we serve on a large church staff or in a small church, God has a unique, personal call for our lives. Vaclav Havel said, "The real test of a man is not when he plays the role that he wants for himself but when he plays the role destiny has for him."[7] Are we fulfilling the life God has called us to, or are we living for our own personal desires?

In one of his most quoted writings, Ralph Waldo Emerson discussed the importance of being original, of not becoming a mere copy of others. He wrote:

> There is a time in every man's education when he arrives at the conviction that...imitation is suicide; that he must take himself for better or worse as is his portion...The power which resides in him is new in nature, and *none but he knows what that is which he can do, nor does he know until he has tried*...Trust thyself: every heart vibrates to that iron string.[8] (emphasis added)

Emerson's understanding of self-reliance is based on each person's innate ability to become better than he currently is, to personally succeed. The leader knows that through Christ, success —fulfilling our calling—is possible. God is working in us to create a grand masterpiece of workmanship. He has created each of us as vessels for His honor and His glory. When God sees us, He sees the completed work of Christ operating in the world.

We are God's "designer originals." We are each individually formed and created to achieve the purpose God has for us. Many leaders feel the easiest way to success and fulfillment is to copy others, but this is far from the plan of God. Each of us has been given the assignment to fulfill our specific mission in life. To accomplish this mission, God has given us unique gifts and talents. To imitate others is suicide and kills who God created us to be. We need to learn from each other so that we do not reinvent the wheel in every ministry; however, we must not imitate others as the easy way to successful ministry. It may be "successful" on the outside, but it is not the plan God intended for us. It is not leadership.

Imitation violates essential uniqueness and damages creativity.[9] When we copy others, we avoid using any creativity. The plans of others have been worked out over time. Sweat, tears, disappointments, and commitment have created their model of ministry. When we imitate the process of others, we do not copy the commitment level of the process. We do not "own" the plan for our churches or our lives because we have not invested in it. This leaves us less committed to the system we are adopting because we have not spent the same amount of effort and energy in creating the system.

Imitation is, at best, a simplified version of the original. It is the synthesized, packaged resource version. Christian bookstores are lined with books on how to grow churches and leaders. Many have boiled down the ten or twenty years of hard work and history of their growth into 250 pages for only $19.99. While these resources may help leaders develop the plan to which God has called them, it is not a one-size-fits-all model for spiritual leadership. No one can show all the bends in the road, the detours that come, or the dangers of the journey. Leaders who copy others are cheap imitations of the original.

Imitation rarely improves on the original product. There is no motivation to increase its effectiveness when the product is already successful. The innovative leader is always looking for new ways to live and operate in ministry. When the leader and the church begin to copy others, their sense of innovation and destiny are lost. For those who copy, it will not be necessary to think big or to create better ways because they can wait until someone else does it and then appropriate their improvements.

In this sense, imitating others means we are always behind the learning curve. When the imitator realizes there is a new way to do ministry, everyone else is already aware of it. The identifying niche of our church and ministry in actuality does not set us apart from others. The niche we copy makes us look exactly like everyone around us.

Why do so many preachers fail to implement their God-given calling in their daily lives and ministry? What is it that keeps them from moving forward in new areas of evangelism? What causes them to become stuck in ministerial ruts for most of their lives? The answer to all of these questions is the *fear of failure*. Fear will take the blue out of our sky and the joy out of our heart. It is fear that dries up the well of innovation and locks the door of implementation. When preachers have completely grasped their divine calling to preach the gospel, many of the insecurities and fears fade away.

There are times in our ministries when the Lord will bring us to fearful situations in order to teach us how to handle them. We will never experience victory over fear until we have to face fearful things. However, we can face these fearful challenges with confidence when we know once and for all that God has called us to the preaching task. God gives us enough grace to fulfill our gift (Ephesians 4:7). Remember that God does not create copies, but He designs originals to accomplish the Great Commission. We must not settle for anything less than complete inner peace regarding our divine call into full-time ministry.

GOD PROVIDENTIALLY DIRECTS OUR LIFE

When we get where we are going, where will we be? The call God places on our life enables us to live without fear of the future. God's providence helps us to see things as He sees them. Moses had the faith to see the invisible (Hebrews 11:27) and that enabled him to see the Promised Land in spite of Pharaoh's threats. As God-called leaders, we must creatively break out of the box around us and approach life through a system of understanding and values that may be foreign to others. Our faith in God allows us to see and operate differently than nonbelievers because, although the context and surroundings are the same, we have a different perspective—a different paradigm.

Vision: The Ability to See the Future

On May 29, 1953, Sir Edmund Hillary raised the British flag atop Mount Everest, becoming the first human being ever to climb to the top of the world. Through sheer walls of ice, lack of oxygen, and bitter cold, Hillary and his companion, Tenzing Norgay, clawed their way between rock and ice to 29,028 feet above sea level. No man on earth will ever climb higher than that. Many have died trying to reach Everest's summit. All who had previously attempted this climb, including Hillary a few years before, had failed. Many believed Everest was not scalable because its twisting rock and dangerous cliffs provided no way of climbing. In fact, no one knew if the body could survive at such high altitudes. The paradigms of the day saw the feat as impossible.

Sir Edmund Hillary, however, lived under a different paradigm—one that saw the climbing of Everest as possible. He saw himself atop Mount Everest with the world at his feet months before he began the actual climb. For Hillary, he had already crossed the ice-capped peak in his heart and mind long before he got there.

Synergistic leaders are visionary. They are imaginative and constantly thinking of new ways to scale the heights. Hillary creatively approached each challenge in climbing the mountain.

His ingenuity allowed him to go farther than anyone had ever gone. Since his remarkable climb, over 1,350 climbers have reached Everest's summit.[10] All leaders have mountains in front of them. The challenge of leadership is to conquer the mountain creatively by following the vision God has placed in their hearts. Like Sir Edmund Hillary, we must see the summit long before we try to conquer it, by beginning with the end in mind. The fulfillment of this vision is our passion and defines our purpose in life.

Laurie Beth Jones says, "You are either living your own mission, or you are living someone else's."[11] On the road to where we are going, either we are accomplishing our own goals or we are accomplishing someone else's. Too many leaders of the church are not following the vision, mission, and goals God has given them. They have been sidetracked and now are led by the whims of someone else. They have been distracted from their calling and are pursuing other visions. When we have visions that are not from God, we pursue avenues that take us farther from His mission and will. These distractions come from listening to other people rather than "seeing" through God's Spirit. Often our own desires lead us down paths that seem to be the "best" for us professionally. These false visions entrap us, but God's true vision empowers us.[12] Because we see with the eyes of the Spirit, we can accomplish more than we ever dreamed possible.

The synergistic church needs a vision for what God can do through it. Leaders help the church hear from God and see the vision God has for it. This vision is often stated through a mission or vision statement. The development of this vision or mission takes much time and prayer. It is not received and crafted in a day or even a week. It is a process where God speaks to the leadership of a church and they carefully translate what God is revealing to them into a strong statement of vision and purpose. A word of caution, however, is needed for the leader. Leaders guide the church through the discovery and development of the

God-given vision; they do not *dictate* what that vision is or is not.

George Barna wrote, "In every one of the growing, healthy churches I have studied, a discernible link has been forged between the spiritual and numerical growth of the congregation and the existence, articulation and widespread ownership of God's ministry by the leaders and participants of the church."[13] To be an effective, healthy church, we must be operating in synergy with the vision God has placed in us because He has called us. This common vision articulates the ministry Barna sees as vital to the growth and health of the churches.

Vision's Development and Effect on Ministry

Caleb lived a life influenced by the vision that was placed within him. He understood that God had called him to be a part of the children of Israel who would take the Promised Land. From the great exodus from Egypt to the conquering of Canaan, Caleb was a source of inspiration and vision. He saw what others did not. In Numbers 13:1–16, Caleb and Joshua joined ten fellow spies sent into Canaan to investigate the land God had promised them. The land they surveyed was full of challenges. The inhabitants of Canaan were giants—strong and numerous, living in the fortified cities of the mountains. The spies reported to the children of Israel that it would be impossible to conquer Canaan because of the giants. However, Caleb saw something different because he was a man of vision. He remembered the God of Israel who had defeated the Egyptians and brought them through the Red Sea. This same God had promised to give them this land. He saw past the challenges; he saw through the eyes of the Spirit.

Stimulated by the courage the vision inspired, Caleb declared that the giants they feared would become the very food of Israel (Numbers 14). Sadly, Israel did not listen or see what Joshua and Caleb saw. In fear and unbelief, they turned away and never set foot in the Promised Land.

Caleb, however, did see his vision fulfilled. After four decades, Joshua and Caleb found themselves at the same place facing the same enemies. The only difference was that they were with a people who were willing to follow a vision and trust in God. At the age of 85, Caleb recalled the promises of God and asked to be allowed to lead the charge against the giants who had prevented them from possessing the promise of God years earlier. Caleb saw what others could not. His strength lay in the vision placed in him by God. What made Caleb so special? As a man of vision, Caleb had already conquered the mountain in his heart. Just like Sir Edmund Hillary, the mountain had already been defeated.

Before we can conquer a mountain with our hand, we must first conquer it in our heart.

Before we can conquer a mountain with our hand, we must first conquer it in our heart. We will never possess the vision God has given us physically until we have possessed it internally. While Caleb wandered with Israel in the wilderness for forty years, the mountain burned within him. He never gave up on conquering the mountain; he could already see its defeat. Synergistic leaders have this kind of vision. Unlike others who are lost in the wilderness, they know they are only walking toward their eventual victory. While others have filled their hearts with compromise and complacency in the wilderness, leaders keep the mountain in their hearts. Caleb had a different paradigm than the rest of Israel. He and Joshua knew what God could do through them; they saw it through the power of God's Spirit.

Caleb's life exemplifies three components of vision. Supernatural vision is birthed by God, is built through challenges, and brings us to victory. Each of these is described below.

Vision Is Birthed by God

Caleb had the courage to believe he could possess the Promised Land. He had the mountain in his heart from the moment he saw it. God had prepared him for this kind of faith. From where did Caleb's vision come? Caleb saw what others did not because his vision was based on God's promises, God's purposes, and God's perspective.

The vision of the mountain was in Caleb's heart because God had promised Israel a land flowing with milk and honey. He promised them that just as He had provided for them in the desert, so would He protect them in the new Promised Land. Caleb knew that the same God who had delivered them from Egypt had promised to fight their battles for them. God has enough power to keep the promises He has made. He never intended for Israel to wander in the wilderness for forty years. He promised Israel the conquest of Canaan; they simply refused to see far enough into the future to trust Him. Visionaries see the future in light of God's promises, and synergistic leaders trust in the promises of God.

Caleb's perspective was different from the other ten spies. He saw the mountain from God's perspective. He was standing on different, higher ground than the other spies. As leaders, we must have a different vantage point than those around us. Some look down at problems rather than looking up at them. Remember the spies' complaint about the giants of Canaan—that they made the Israelites feel like "grasshoppers." Many people fall victim to the grasshopper complex: they always seem small and the trials of life always seem big. They always look up at the enemy instead of looking down on their problems. Israel made the mistake of comparing themselves to their problem rather than comparing their problem to God. They were willing to believe that they could not do it, rather than believing that, through them, God could do all things. Because God was the source of

Caleb's vision, he did not fear the giants. They seemed small in comparison to his God, and he saw them with a different perspective. This same vision was in the shepherd boy, David, as he faced the giant, Goliath. He, too, was not afraid of the enemy because of his view of God.

Many years ago, I (Bill) was greatly challenged with the reports of the ten disobedient spies. They felt like grasshoppers in their own view of themselves. I determined not to be a "grasshopper" and preached several sermons on that subject. I realized that God's power, wisdom, and love are so great that we are limited only by our own view of ourselves and our lack of faith in Him. We will not see ourselves as grasshoppers but as valiant warriors when we fight with God on our side.

There are all kinds of giants challenging the church, but God is bigger than the giants. There will be some who will see the problems as too big; and just like the ten spies with the grasshopper complex, they will return to the wilderness and die. Rather than looking up at the obstacles, we must have a heavenly perspective and look down on the giants in our path. Even giants seem like ants when we are looking from heaven.

God was the source of Caleb's vision. Caleb understood that Canaan belonged to the Lord. This is where the visioning of the secular, corporate world and the church world diverge. As leaders, we do not create vision; we receive vision. This does not imply a lack of creativity on our part but acknowledges the source of all spiritual vision—God. Because God has called us, we must not be satisfied with the status quo. We see what can be accomplished through the eyes of the Holy Spirit, and we must see the vision fulfilled.

What vision has God given us? Can we easily state the mission of our life? If so, what kinds of obstacles are in our path? Do we view them from a biblical perspective, or do we suffer from the grasshopper complex?

Vision Is Built Through Challenges

The capture of Caleb's mountain would not be easy. Vision does not candy-coat the future. Although Caleb saw the giants from God's perspective, they were still giants. Vision does not see things that do not exist or make difficult things disappear. Caleb saw the same giants, walled cities, and mountain ranges the other spies saw; however, his vision was not limited to the physical realm. Conquering Canaan would be a difficult but not an impossible task. Caleb knew that, most likely, some Israelites would die in the battles required to possess the land of promise; but he also knew that the God of Israel had promised to fight for them. Leaders are aware of the challenges ahead and are willing to face them because they know God will be with them. They survey the journey and see the obstacles in their way. The challenges that lie ahead only serve to strengthen the vision, and the vision stirs up courage in the heart of the visionaries.

Just like Caleb, leaders face challenges. Though others around them may doubt, leaders know that it is God who makes the impossible possible. With vision, they see past the current situation to the end where God allows them to possess the promise He has for them. The challenges they face are there to build the vision inside them. These challenges are the stepping-stones along the path that strengthen the visionary for the final destination. God has a purpose in every stage of the journey, even the bumps in the road. These challenges may look like giants to some, but they are small in comparison to the God who gives us the vision to accomplish the mission He has called us to do.

Vision Brings Us to Victory

Caleb was forced to postpone conquering the mountain God had placed in his heart because of the failure of Israel. When Caleb finally saw his vision come to fulfillment, he was 85 years old. After wandering in the wilderness, Caleb found himself at the foot of the same giant-filled mountain that had frightened the children of Israel forty years before. Listen to his words to Joshua:

> Now behold, the LORD has let me live, just as He spoke, these forty-five years, from the time that the LORD spoke this word to Moses, when Israel walked in the wilderness; and now behold, I am eighty-five years old today.
>
> I am still as strong today as I was in the day Moses sent me; as my strength was then, so my strength is now, for war and for going out and coming in.
>
> Now then, give me this hill country about which the LORD spoke on that day, for you heard on that day that Anakim were there, with great fortified cities; perhaps the LORD will be with me, and I will drive them out as the LORD has spoken (Joshua 14:10–12).

The mountain was still in Caleb's heart! The very mountain that caused others to turn back was the motivator for Caleb's perseverance. His vision was about to become reality. How did he keep that mountain in his heart for forty years in the desert?

The vision God gave Caleb inspired him to undying faith. His faith did not diminish in the wilderness. Through his forty long years of circling in the desert, the image of a conquered mountain only grew stronger. There is no way of knowing how many times Caleb fought and captured the walled cities of those mountains in his heart while walking in the desert. *Let others die in the wilderness if they want to, but we are going to take the mountain.* He never gave up on the promised vision in front of him. Everything he did was in preparation for accomplishing the vision. When the going gets tough, leaders rely upon the vision God places in them for faith.

Though Caleb had not possessed the land physically, he had possessed the mountain in his heart. There are two ways to possess something: in your heart and in your hands. Even wandering in the wilderness could not take the mountain away from Caleb. He had already possessed it through the power of vision.

Do we have a mountain in our heart? Do we live in victory while in the wilderness? While we are in the wilderness, we must never lose sight of the mountain in our heart. It will sustain us on our journey just like Caleb. A God-inspired vision allows leaders to walk in faith, devotion, and strength until they reach their goal.

In 1945, God gave me (Bill) a vision for a film on the life of Christ. It was necessary to persevere and not give up. The vision for the *JESUS* film, an instrument of evangelism that would impact over 6 billion people, took thirty-five years to become a reality. Because it may take time before our visions become reality, we must never let the vision leave our hearts.

Pursuing Our Vision

People of vision see what others cannot. Though others cannot make sense of the situation, it seems normal to leaders. God has birthed in them a vision that has been strengthened by challenges and will bring them to victory. They see how events are falling into place while others think they are falling apart. Their perspective is different; their current surroundings are the raw material of the future vision. They may be in the wilderness now, but the mountain is in their hearts.

The leaders of the synergistic church live a life of faith and trust in God. They see the end of the journey and allow God to guide them on the path. In 1951, God placed the vision for Campus Crusade for Christ in my heart. If we had been told then that from the UCLA campus would be birthed an organization that by 2001 would have more than 27,000 full-time staff and more than 600,000 trained volunteers, that we would help to start more than 750,000 churches and expose more than 6 billion people to the gospel, we would not have believed it. God reveals His vision for our lives in increments that we can handle and builds our faith to help us accomplish that vision.

The mountain God placed in our hearts has grown as we have learned to trust Him. He began, however, by showing us what we could do and continue to do—reach university students for Jesus Christ. Our slogan from the beginning has been, "Win the campus to Christ today; win the world to Christ tomorrow." God gave a vision of what could be; and through His power, we are attempting to make it a reality.

What is preventing us from realizing our potential, from accomplishing the vision God has given us? Are there doubts, discouragements, or distractions in our life? Do we feel like a grasshopper beneath the giant foot of adversity? Through the power of vision, we must see what others cannot. We must see the fulfillment of the promises of God in our life and see challenges as the building blocks of the future. We must possess the mountain in our heart.

Florence Chadwick was the first woman to swim the English Channel in both directions. She set records around the world for great feats of long-distance swimming. At the age of 34, her goal was to become the first woman to swim from Catalina Island to the California coast. On July 4, 1952, in freezing water and intense fog, she set out to accomplish this daring feat. For sixteen hours, she swam in fog so thick she could barely see the support boats that followed her. Several times sharks were driven away by rifle fire. Within half a mile of the shore, she asked to be pulled from the water. Her trainer assured her she could make it the final half mile, but all she could see was fog. In an interview after the swim, she said, "I'm not excusing myself, but if I could have seen the land, I might have made it." Two months later with the shore clearly pictured in her heart and mind, she attempted and accomplished the swim. What was the difference? She had a clear vision of the shore, and that was her strength.

Through the power of the Holy Spirit, leaders enable people to see what they cannot see on their own. They help people see the shore ahead even when it is clouded by mist and fog. They help people realize that the mountain God has promised must first be conquered in their hearts. We are living our own vision and helping others discover their vision.

CONCLUSION

While the call of God is specific and personal, at times it may be hard to find. The journey of God's calling may be filled with false paths, experiments, and setbacks and require practice and prayer.[14] If you are uncertain about your calling to be a minister of the Lord Jesus Christ, spend some quality time with some of God's choicest servants. Make plans soon to set quality time aside and search your soul regarding the call of God for your life. If you are waiting until the pressures of ministry subside before resolving this important issue, you may have to wait the rest of your life. In this case, waiting time could be wasted time. It may take several years to know for certain that the calling rests upon your life.

As you are led by the Spirit of God to fulfill the calling of God on your life, you will experience His power and purpose at work in you. You will be inspired by the vision that He has given you so that, like Caleb, you can defeat the mountains in your heart before you even face them. Vision, calling, and power go hand in hand. God faithfully enables you through His Holy Spirit. It is important to understand that unless you know that you are called by God and are empowered by the Holy Spirit, you cannot reach a level of significance and fruitfulness in your ministry. Unless you fulfill that calling, avoiding the distraction of imitation, you will never achieve all God has for you in ministry and in life.

CHAPTER 5

Character Developed by God

A Columbine High School student accurately summed up today's culture in a communication on the Internet during the fall of 1999. The words are filled with a need for a consistent world:

> The paradox of our time in history is that we have taller buildings but shorter tempers, wider freeways but narrower viewpoints.
>
> We spend more but have less; we buy more but enjoy less.
> We have bigger houses but smaller families, more conveniences but less time.
> We have more degrees but less sense, more knowledge but less judgment, more experts but more problems, more medicine but less wellness.
>
> We have multiplied our possessions but *reduced our values.*
> We talk too much, love too seldom, and hate too often.
> We have learned how to make a living but not a life.

We have added years to life but not life to years.
We have been all the way to the moon and back but have
trouble crossing the street to meet the new neighbor.
We have conquered outer space but not inner space.

We have cleaned up the air but have polluted the soul.
We have split the atom but not our prejudices.
We have higher incomes *but lower morals.*
We have become long on quantity but short on quality.

These are the times of tall men *but short character*; steep
profits, shallow relationships.
These are the times of world peace but domestic warfare,
more leisure but less fun, more kinds of food but less
nutrition.
These are the days of two incomes but more divorce, of
fancier houses but broken homes.

It is a time when *there is much in the show window and
nothing in the stockroom*, a time when technology can
bring this letter to you, and a time when you can
choose either to make a difference…or just hit delete.
(emphasis added)

Sadly, when it comes to the issue of character, most of us hit delete. Our world is cruel and brutal. The things that used to make us weep now make us laugh. The awful effects of sin have seared the conscience of our culture. We no longer govern according to what is right and wrong but according to what works and what makes money. Our culture has sold its soul to materialism, filled nearly every sector with liberalism, and has as its theme, "If it feels good, do it."

The church must stand against the attacks of the enemy. We must stand firmly consistent in a world that embraces moral relativism and abandons conscience and love. We must see God moving among the chaos of the world. Where others see death, real leaders see the potential for life. We are not bound by temporal circumstances because we can see the eternal Creator. We see the potential in all people for knowing Christ and changing the world. People focused on the present world see the pleasures, treasures, and measures of the world, not the potential of Christ working in it (1 John 2:16). John says that in the world there are the "cravings of sinful man"—the world's *pleasures*. The person who is distracted by sin cannot focus on the Savior. God's Word says that in the world there is "the lust of the eyes" —the *treasures* of the world. Worldly people desire the temporary beauty of the earth rather than the eternal beauty of heaven. The Bible also says the world is filled with the "boasting of what man has and does"—the *measures* of the world. Worldly people trust in their accomplishments for advancements instead of boasting in the work of the cross. Worldly people cannot see the invisible world because they look only at the present world. Moses did not have a worldly view. He was able to look ahead and see the invisible reward because he trusted in God despite his circumstances (Hebrews 11:26,27). His eyes were on the Creator, not the attractions of the world.

We must rise up and help make a difference in the world. When the roof is removed from the church, our lives are laid open before God. We see Him in all His glory, and He sees us in all that we say and do. With the image of a powerful, loving God above us, we cannot help but live our lives in surrender to Him. The moral fiber of the synergistic church must be strong. Our character must match the volume of our rhetoric. Many people *tell* others what to do and how to do it. We must *show* people what to do through our godly actions and our Christlike character.

The Christian life must be lived in total, absolute surrender to our great God and Savior. We surrender to the lordship of Jesus Christ, becoming His bondservants or slaves to His will and desires. The act of surrender strengthens our character, and our character enables us not only to live holy lives but also to persevere through the trials and adversities of life. We finish the course before us. Living a consistent life means we are committed to hard work. The difference between an effective, fruitful ministry for Christ and a mediocre ministry is hard work in the power of the Holy Spirit. God's Word commands us "to work hard as unto the Lord" (Colossians 3:23). Paul said, "I can *do* [not "I can sit or wait"] all things through Christ which strengtheneth me" (Philippians 4:13, KJV, emphasis added). It is a principle that is only understood when seen through the eyes of potential. As leaders, we are not afraid to work hard or go the extra mile because we see what can happen from our hard work in the Lord.

INTEGRITY AND CONSISTENCY
IN OUR ACTIONS

When we live with our lives open to our marvelous, glorious God, our only alternative is to live a holy life of integrity and consistency. In the spring of 1951, Vonette and I (Bill) signed a contract to become slaves of Jesus Christ, renouncing everything to the control of our Lord Jesus Christ. We assumed the position of bond slaves, a role exemplified in the obedient life of our Lord Jesus Christ (Philippians 2:7). In the contract, Vonette and I relinquished everything we owned or ever would own to Him. We dedicated ourselves to our Lord, Master, Savior, and King, and entered into a Galatians 2:20 relationship. The vision for Campus Crusade for Christ came approximately twenty-four hours after the signing of this contract. We believe we would not have received this vision if we had not first surrendered our lives totally, completely, and irrevocably to the lordship of Christ. The phenomenal results have been the work of our master—to Him be all glory and praise.

Leaders must submit themselves to the lordship of Jesus Christ. You, too, might want to make a contract with our Lord.

It has been a source of great strength and liberation for Vonette and me as well as many other families. When we surrender to the lordship of Christ, we follow Him in all that we do. He molds and shapes our lives, and we live for Him alone. As a result, we are conformed into His image.

Surrendering to the Lordship of Christ

One of the dangers of being a Christian leader is the misuse of authority. We must never forget that we are called to serve. If we are not careful, we forget that the source of our leadership is Jesus Christ. We are reminded of Paul's words, "I glory in Christ Jesus in my service to God" (Romans 15:17, NIV). As leaders, we must keep in mind that we serve those we are called to lead and that we live our lives in submission to the lordship of Christ. Too many times, pastors fail because they become greater in their own eyes than they really are. They believe the compliments people give them. They assume that success and position give them privilege and license to do whatever they choose. Solomon warns us, "When pride comes, then comes dishonor, but with the humble is wisdom" (Proverbs 11:2). The leader who presides arrogantly over the church rebuilds the roof between himself and God. Our own pride is usually the major factor preventing us from surrendering to Jesus Christ. Pride becomes a limit we must move beyond.

The path of surrender takes three steps. To really surrender to Christ, we must break our pride, bow in humility, and bear our cross. When we follow these steps, we can prevent our character from being called into question, especially in the arena of leadership. Leaders must constantly remember to fight the fleshly nature within them and to follow these steps to become a slave of Jesus Christ. Many individuals in positions of leadership or those aspiring to leadership roles have sensed a desire to make a significant mark with their lives and work. This motivation often comes from a sincere desire to serve Christ and His Church. We must be careful, however, to understand that any success that happens in ministry is only because Christ has chosen us to accomplish *His* plan. Jesus said, "Apart from Me you can do nothing" (John 15:5). To avoid the pride that leads to a downfall in the life of the leader and to always remain a slave of Jesus Christ, we must follow these three steps:

Break our pride. Pride seems to be one of the constant components of every human personality that irresistibly begins to drive us early in life.[1] The slave of Jesus Christ has nothing to boast about but Jesus Christ, because we have submitted everything to God. We are to give our entire body as a tool for the glory of God, available for His use and the worship of Him (Romans 6:13). In the hands of the construction worker, the hammer never looks back at a finished house and thinks, "My, what a great hammer I am. Look at the house I built!" The hammer is just the tool. The effort, the ingenuity, and the credit go to the builder. This same principle applies to our lives. We are the tools God uses in leadership. Even in success, we have nothing about which to boast or be proud. God is the one who deserves all the glory and honor for the accomplishment.

Bow in humility. Paul encourages believers to be "slaves of Christ, doing the will of God from the heart" (Ephesians 6:6). We must submit our will to Christ. If we follow our own desires and path, we no longer serve Christ as Lord. Jesus is the perfect example of one who submitted His will to God. "I have come down from heaven, not to do My own will, but the will of Him who sent Me" (John 6:38). Submission is not a popular concept today, but our ability to submit to God determines whether we struggle through life or really live. Jesus submitted to His Father even to the point of going to the cross. As Paul admonished, we must bow before Christ and offer ourselves as living sacrifices:

> Therefore I urge you, brethren, by the mercies of God, to present your bodies a living and holy sacrifice, accept-

able to God, which is your spiritual service of worship.

And do not be conformed to this world, but be transformed by the renewing of your mind, so that you may prove what the will of God is, that which is good and acceptable and perfect (Romans 12:1,2).

In humility, we should acknowledge the lordship of Christ over our lives and the ministry He has given us. We must renounce our personal desires, needs, rights, and accomplishments.

Bear our cross. Many people are more interested in wearing a cross than bearing a cross. Jesus said, "If anyone wishes to come after Me, he must deny himself, and take up his cross and follow Me" (Mark 8:34). The essence of life as a slave is found in those last two words: "follow Me."

Leadership positions can easily rob us of our time with God. Leadership titles will tempt us to assert our own authority in different situations. Therefore, leaders can never leave the feet of Jesus. They must lead from a position of dependence on God. When we are dependent on Him, He will use us to further His kingdom. Leaders must never forget they are merely the tools God is using to build His kingdom. Paul admonishes us, "He who boasts is to boast in the LORD" (2 Corinthians 10:17).

Conforming to the Image of Christ

Charles William Eliot (1834–1926), former president of Harvard University, had a birthmark on his face that bothered him greatly. As a young man, he was told that surgeons could do nothing to remove it.

Someone described that moment as "the dark hour of his soul." Eliot's mother gave him helpful advice: "My son, it is not possible for you to get rid of that hardship...But it is possible for you, with God's help, to grow a mind and a soul so big that people will forget to look at your face." Peter wrote about the beauty of "the hidden person of the heart" (1 Peter 3:4). Although he was speaking to women, the attractiveness of inner spiritual traits is equally becoming to men. Christlike character is more desirable than the finest external physical features.[2] The streams of life flow from our inner heart. And at the heart of one who ministers must be character. Financier J. P. Morgan once commented that "a man's best collateral is his character."[3]

While the character question applies to the leader of the church, it is also for everyone. The synergistic church must strive to make stronger, more mature Christians through discipleship programs. In fact, we are called as leaders to equip the Body of Christ for service. The minister's *purpose* is clearly defined in Paul's letter to the Ephesians. Paul lists the fivefold ministry gifts of the church, which are for the equipping of God's people for the "work of service, to the building up of the body of Christ" (Ephesians 4:11, 12). The purpose of the leader is to equip the church.

> As Christ inhabits our humanity, we are to display His deity more and more.

The Greek term for "equipping" means "to put right" or "to put in order."[4] Equipping denotes "the bringing of the saints to a condition of fitness for the discharge of their functions in the Body, without implying restoration from a disordered state."[5] The church leader is to set the church in order, making each member fit for the work of ministry. The Greek term for "building up" refers "to the act of building . . . to build on something, to build further."[6] We are to help God's people conform to the image of Christ, to help them through the Spirit of God to become people of strong character.

After ministry's purpose—equipping—is established, Paul delineates the *priorities* of the gospel minister. There is a fourfold equipping or maturing function for the leader of the church. To function biblically, their message, motives, methods, and ministry must align with the Christ-given purposes outlined in Ephesians 4:13–16.

The Christian is to become mature in *stature*. We must be active "until we all attain to the unity of the faith, and of the knowledge of the Son of God, to a mature man, to the measure of the stature which belongs to the fullness of Christ" (v. 13). This verse paints a picture of the Church maturing "into a perfect, full-grown man." The whole Body of Christ is viewed as one new man with one faith in the Son of God. The "faith" is the full message of the gospel. The "measure of the stature" indicates a level of spiritual perfection found in the fullness of Christ. The Body of Christ is seen as progressing toward its future goal of perfection in the fullness of Christ. In short, as Christ inhabits our humanity, we are to display His deity more and more as we are being conformed to His image.

Second, we must help others become mature in *stability*. The apostle Paul writes, "As a result, we are no longer to be children, tossed here and there by waves, and carried about by every wind of doctrine, by the trickery of men, by craftiness in deceitful scheming" (v. 14). In verses 13 and 14, there is a purposeful contrast made between "a perfect full-grown man" and "children." Instead of spiritual maturity, the picture is of "spiritual infantilism." The concept that Paul teaches is not of physical infants in a boat who are helpless to manage it in wind and waves, but of physical men who know nothing about managing boats and are as infants amid wind and waves.

Paul warns of dangerous preaching that comes from "the trickery of men" and by their "craftiness in deceitful scheming." Those who preach this false doctrine are seen as willfully undermining the Body of Christ. These tricksters appeal to the immature Christian who is often deceived by unethical tactics and persuasive words. Leaders must take full responsibility for their message, methods, and motives in ministry. Their ethics and exhortations must cause the Body of Christ to be stable in an unstable world.

Third, we can help the local church become more mature in *speech*. The apostle Paul continues, "Speaking the truth in love, we are to grow up in all *aspects* into Him, who is the head, *even* Christ" (v. 15, emphasis added). "Speaking the truth" means "truthing" or "doing the truth."[7] Mature Christians recognize the lies of religious tricksters by comparing them to the truth. They correct the error of these religious charlatans by speaking the truth in love. "Truthing in love" keeps "every joint" (v. 16) limber and flexible in the midst of a changing culture. It has been said, "Whatever is in the well of the heart comes out in the bucket of speech." When the heart of the Body of Christ is filled with truth and love, Christians will lovingly confront all error in their society.

Fourth, we equip the local church to mature in *service*. Paul writes, "From whom the whole body, being fitted and held together by what every joint supplies, according to the proper working of each individual part, causes the growth of the body for the building up of itself in love" (v. 16). The ultimate goal of an active, fivefold ministry is to have each member fulfilling his or her role. The whole body of Christ is being "fitted together" and "held together" by each separate "joint." It is only when every member is working together in synergy that the Body of Christ receives the full support it needs to do the "work of service." The lifeblood of the Body of Christ is "love." Each member is to have a loving heart toward the other members of the Body of Christ.

PERSEVERING THROUGH TRIALS

Character is not just a matter of doing the right things; it is also staying consistent through adversity. Perseverance is a word seldom heard anymore. Our society is being programmed to want everything faster. If an activity requires time and effort, it is not worth doing. We must fulfill the calling God has placed on our lives even in the hard times. We must live lives of integrity and consistency, persevering even when it is difficult to do so.

Going the Second Mile

Among the many principles taught by Jesus Christ, the principle of "the second mile" completely highlights the dynamics of true discipleship. In the middle of the Sermon on the Mount, Jesus said, "Whoever shall force you to go one mile, go with him two" (Matthew 5:4). It is the second-mile principle that will put a smile on our face, a spring in our step, and a song in our heart. The first mile is the trial mile, and the second is the smile mile. The key to living life with a smile is a Christ-centered life.

There are several reasons for going the second mile as a leader in the synergistic church. The second mile is *the character mile*. What was Jesus talking about when He said, "Whoever shall force you to go one mile, go with him two"? In Jesus' day, the Romans had a practice that they had learned from the Persians about six hundred years earlier. This practice was to subjugate the people who had been conquered through war. A Roman soldier could command a Jewish man or boy to carry his backpack or burden for one mile. The Jewish person was required by law to oblige. Most Jews in this situation would carry the burden the requisite mile and not one inch more. The law caused terrible resentment among the Jews toward the Roman government.

Can you imagine how the Jews felt when Jesus said, "Go the second mile"? The audience no doubt said, "He must be joking. Carry the burden for the Romans an extra mile? Who does He think He is? The law says only one mile, not two." It would be hard for most people to do more than the law required of them. Jesus was calling for ministry over and above the requirements. He was looking for people filled with love and servanthood.

Jesus was looking for second-milers.

Second-milers do more than is required or expected. Jesus showed that any pagan or unsaved person could go one mile (Matthew 5:46,47). The first mile is to love those who love us. The second mile is to love those who do not love us. When a Jew was carrying the soldier's burden for the first mile, he was a slave. However, when he chose to carry the burden for a second mile, he then took control of the situation. The character mile moves us from slaves to masters. The first mile is the "have-to" mile, but the second mile is the "want-to" mile.

The second mile is *the commitment mile*. We go the first mile out of legalism but continue the second mile out of love. In order to live like Jesus, we must go the second mile when we experience *personal degradation* (Matthew 5:38,39). The first mile is to give place to revenge, but the second mile is to give place to love. Jesus said, "Whoever slaps you on your right cheek, turn to him the other also" (v. 39). In order for someone to strike us on the right cheek, that person must hit us with the back of the hand. If someone has treated us disrespectfully before others, this is an appropriate opportunity to go the second mile. As Abraham Lincoln stated, the best way to get rid of an enemy is to make that enemy a friend.

Furthermore, the commitment mile includes *personal defeat*. In Matthew 5:40, Jesus is talking about a legal settlement in which a brother has been found guilty. He is required to give his shirt. Jesus is saying that if we know we have done wrong, we should not simply try to rectify the wrong by fulfilling the law, but we should also go the second mile. If we are wrong, then we need to apologize, make things right with our brother and God, and then go the second mile.

Not only does the second mile include personal degradation and personal defeat, but also *personal dedication* (Matthew 5:42). We are to have a giving spirit. We are not simply to pay our bills but also give to those who are in real need. In order to live like

Jesus, we go the second mile when others have wronged us, when we have wronged others, and when there are serious financial needs.

Last, the second mile is *the commission mile*. Successful people live by the second-mile principle. The first mile is crowded, but the second mile is not busy at all. Imagine two different scenes. In the first scene, a Roman soldier commands a Jewish man to carry his burden for an entire mile. The man becomes extremely upset as he picks up the soldier's burden and begins to carry it. As he does so, he mutters in angry tones at the soldier. At the end of a mile, he throws the burden down and returns home, full of rage, hatred, and anger.

The second scene is the complete opposite of the first. As soon as the Roman soldier commands the Jewish man to carry his burden, the Jew responds with a warm, friendly greeting. In his heart, he truly wants to win this soldier to the Lord. Along the way, he converses with the soldier. At the end of the first mile, the Jewish man says, "If you do not mind, I would be honored to carry your burden for a second mile."

Can you imagine the incredulous look on the soldier's face when he hears these words? The Roman soldier might say, "There is something different about you. Most Jews become angry when I command them to carry my backpack. What makes you different from the others?" The Jewish man says, "On one occasion, I heard Jesus Christ teach on the second-mile principle, so I am doing what He commanded me to do." The soldier responds, "Who is Jesus Christ?" The Jewish man answers, "He is the Messiah, the Savior of the world."

By the time they reach the end of the second mile, the Jewish man has shared the gospel with the Roman soldier. The second mile is the witnessing mile. More souls would be saved if we lived our lives on the second mile. Jesus went the second mile for all of us. Why would anyone want to live on the trial mile when we can live on the smile mile?

121

Learning to Stand When We Do Not Understand

In the 1990s, my wife, Sheri, and I (James) spent a lot of time in the Greenlawn North Cemetery in Springfield, Missouri. Greenlawn North is a beautiful cemetery where maple trees create a magnificent show of vibrant colors in the fall. It is like a gorgeous park where many walk and run throughout the year. Our first pictures while we were dating were taken there in October 1982. We never imagined that our two precious children, Jennifer and James, would be born, live such short times, and then die in Sheri's arms in the Cox South Medical Center and be laid to rest at Greenlawn. Jennifer and James were born at 24½ and 29 weeks of gestation in 1991 and 1998, respectively. Our daughter lived for six weeks; and our baby son, born on Valentine's Day, died the following day. Even though we know our children are with Christ, the pain of helplessly watching our babies—with tiny features already resembling ours—die and burying them side by side was devastating to us.

On a spring afternoon in 1998, I stood by our children's graves pondering the most important priorities in life. As I read both the birth and passing dates on their tombstones, I began to reflect on the millions of children who are born each year around the world. Many are born into a Christless culture with very little hope of finding eternal life. If we do not have a worldwide spiritual awakening, the children will suffer the most in the years ahead. They will mature in a culture that has long forgotten the ways of the Lord.

How do we continue to serve God when we have trials like this in our life? How do we continue in spite of the questions that plague us when we come to major trials? The prophet Habakkuk faced such a time in his life. The king of Babylon had conquered Palestine, and Jerusalem was plundered. Promising young men like Daniel, Shadrach, Meshach, and Abednego had been taken away while untold thousands were killed. Habakkuk wrestled to understand the ways of God. He agonized in prayer for answers. To Habakkuk, it seemed that God was silent in the face of their adversity (Habakkuk 1:2). In addition, God appeared not to care that the righteous of Israel were suffering. The wicked Babylonians seemed to be prospering at the expense of Israel. God responded to Habakkuk with a revelation that works its way through Scripture: "The just [righteous] shall live by faith" (Habakkuk 2:4, KJV). There are three components to that phrase: the just, shall live, and by faith. Interestingly, this phrase occurs three times in Scripture. In Romans 5:1, Paul writes that it is by faith that we have been justified and have obtained peace with God. In Hebrews 10:38, the author reminds us that the righteous will live by faith. In each of these sections, a different component is emphasized. Habakkuk is concerned about the righteous. He cannot understand why Israel is facing so much hardship. His questions sounded something like, "God, we are serving you, but all these bad things are happening and it does not make sense." God points out to Habakkuk that it is He who makes the righteous just, and it is the ability to live by faith that makes them righteous.

Many children are born into a Christless culture with very little hope of finding eternal life.

Paul's concern is the living part of the righteous person's life. This quote is couched between instructions on holy living. It is not enough just to have faith; we must live it out and actively pursue what we have inside of us. The Book of Hebrews is teaching on faith. Hebrews 10:38 precedes Hebrews 11, the great chapter on faith. When each occurrence is viewed together, we realize that we must depend on God in every aspect of our lives. We must trust in Him to lead us through adversity. We are not sinful for asking questions of God—only human. It is a sign of character that we live through trials by faith. When we understand the love and faithfulness of God, we can rejoice and give thanks no matter what our circumstances (James 1; Romans 5; and 1 Thessalonians 5:18). When we do that as an expression of faith, Jesus reveals Himself to us (John 14:21).

FINISHING THE RACE: REALIZING OUR POTENTIAL

Within each Christian leader—indeed, within every one of God's children—lies the ability to transform a community, a nation, and the world. Oliver Wendell Holmes once said that most people die with the music still in them. They never let out what God has put in them. Their song was never heard because they did not know its potential. People of character are people who are hard-working. They finish the race they are asked to run.

When we live our lives beyond the limitations of ineffectiveness and unfulfillment, we come to several realizations. These are very important to the workings of the synergistic church, and they are important to integrate into the local church.

Leaders realize there are no shortcuts to long-term effectiveness.

"If building a great church were easy, there would be a lot of great churches." This summary of church leadership came from a discussion with George Sawyer, a pastor in Decatur, Alabama. His words have captivated me (James) for several months. After joining with his church in worship and evangelism, I had commented on how great a church he pastored. The above response has stuck with me ever since. All of the ideas, thoughts, creativity, and even potential amount to little if they are not acted upon. The greatest enemy to church growth is not a satanic attack but the laziness of the flesh. Too many leaders are looking for shortcuts to success, and there are no shortcuts in ministry if we want to be effective. While many long for successful ministries, it is the leaders who work hard over time, drawing upon the mighty power of God, who ultimately grow the greatest churches. While we cannot all be great, we can all at least be effective.[8]

George Washington Carver, a former slave, is considered one of the world's greatest agricultural scientists. This self-educated African-American discovered more than 300 byproducts of peanuts, sweet potatoes, and soybeans. He received many awards for discoveries that affect our lives even today. Carver tells of a pivotal moment in his development. His foster parents were on a trip for several weeks, and Carver decided to help at home by repairing, cleaning, and polishing items in the house. When his parents returned, Carver proudly listed all of his achievements. Mariah, his foster mother, interrupted, "Now, George, don't tell me the number of things you have done but how well you have done them." It was a lesson he always remembered. This same work ethic continued throughout his life. While teaching at the Tuskegee Institute, he initiated strict rules for his students. He did not tolerate laziness or underachievement. Assignments not 100 percent completed or on time were rejected. He hated projects that were "about" finished and often told his students, "Remember, the more ignorant we are, the less use God has for us. There are only two ways. One is right and the other is wrong. "About" is always wrong. Don't tell me it's about right. If it's only about right, then it's wrong. If you come to a stream five feet wide and jump four and a half feet, you fall in and drown."[9] Carver was able to accomplish great things because he was willing to work harder than most. Carver drew this work ethic not only from family but also from God's Word. He had a profound faith in Christ and daily sought God's wisdom and guidance.

Many people comment on how large Campus Crusade for Christ has grown. When they tour the facilities or see the number of people who have been introduced to Christ, they marvel at how this incredible ministry "just came into existence." Campus Crusade for Christ did not "just happen." These last fifty years have been a constant struggle of Spirit-empowered perspiration. The sweat, tears, and prayers of thousands of workers have developed Campus Crusade into a worldwide evangelistic ministry. This is not the work of Vonette and Bill Bright but of thousands of these glorious individuals who have poured themselves into the work of Christ with us. They were determined, as was I, to provide the necessary practical help for making the difference in ministry between mere desire and true effectiveness. They epitomized a phrase I have always sought to exercise in my life: "Inspiration without perspiration leads to frustration and ultimately to stagnation." Yet the most important contribution to the success of this ministry is our Lord Jesus Christ who lives in each staff member. The staff know the reality that it is not what we do for Christ that counts, but what He does in and through us.

Leaders realize that if they do not follow through, they have not really followed their calling.

When God told Israel to conquer Canaan, He promised them He would give them every place they set their foot (Joshua 1:3). He gave them specific instructions to possess the whole land and not let anyone remain (vv. 4,5). As Joshua led them across Canaan, they destroyed every town except Gaza, Gath, and Ashdod. For some reason, they allowed survivors in these towns (11:22).

This lack of complete victory would haunt Israel in years to come. They did not follow through on what God told them to do. When leaders leave unfinished business in ministry, that unfinished business can finish their ministry. It may not happen immediately, but eventually the "enemies" we fail to conquer will attempt to conquer us.

These Philistine cities and their presence caused much death and destruction throughout the history of Israel and Judah. They constantly caused problems for the children of Israel, who failed to finish the conquest of Canaan. Goliath the giant came from Gath (1 Samuel 17:4). Is it a coincidence that the antagonist of Israel came from one of the cities spared in the conquest of Canaan? Goliath provided a political challenge for Israel, and the armies of the Philistines came through Gath.

It was in the Philistine city of Gaza that Samson, the great judge, met Delilah and fell victim to her temptations. As a seaport, Gaza provided many temptations and trials for the children of Israel, and was a place of moral challenge. When leaders do not finish the work they are called to do and completely destroy the hold the enemy has in their lives, the unfinished work will tempt them to fall.

The final Philistine city that Joshua's men did not destroy was Ashdod. When the Philistines captured the Ark of the Covenant, they took it to Ashdod (1 Samuel 5:1). Ashdod, which contained a great temple to Dagon, the Philistine god, was a spiritual challenge for Israel. When we do not fulfill the mission God calls us to do and we do not completely finish the task, the Ashdods that remain standing can steal the very presence of God from us. They become places of worship that are not ordained by God.

Leaders realize they are only as effective as the generation that follows them.

It has been reported that Martin Luther once said, "You will know whether or not your life was significant 500 years after you have died." Leaders take the long view, not the short view. Have you considered what your legacy will be? According to Max DePree, a legacy results from the facts of our behavior that remain in the minds of others, the cumulative informal record of how close we came to the person we intended to be.[10]

This is not about setting and achieving goals but establishing and nurturing relationships. People with changed lives are the greatest legacy of a leader. In leadership conferences and in his personal study, John Maxwell has discovered that four out of five leaders emerged because of the impact made on them by a mentor.[11] Leaders lead for tomorrow, not for today. They understand that the best years of the church and their ministry are ahead, not behind. They influence tomorrow by investing in people today.

Real leaders find young leaders and train them for the future. They instill in them values, character, and the tenacity to accomplish their own goals. They replicate themselves over and over again in order to achieve the greatest impact. The leader must invest energy and time into future leaders. It is more than lunches and thirty-minute sharing sessions. Often it is a lifetime of sharing tears, laughter, ideas, and hurts with someone. A legacy is created only when leaders put their organization in the position to do great things without them.[12]

CHAPTER 6

Committed to God

I t is not enough to receive God's call on your life and have your character formed by Christ. We must also demonstrate our commitment to God. The world is filled with people who claim to be committed but who do not follow through. Paul understood the necessity of being fully committed to Christ. Speaking to the Galatians, he wrote, "I have been crucified with Christ, and it is no longer I who live, but Christ lives in me; and the life which I now live in the flesh I live by faith in the Son of God, who loved me and delivered Himself up for me" (2:20). It was this same kind of commitment that led Vonette and me (Bill) to make our contract to become slaves of Jesus Christ. Signing the contract was our act of commitment to God. Since then, we continue to renounce every single thing in our lives—our time, talents, and treasures—to the control of the Lord Jesus Christ. We made a total, absolutely irrevocable commitment to God, and we have been attempting to fulfill that commitment through His grace ever since.

When heaven is laid open before us, our only response is to commit our lives to God. We obey His commands and become like Peter and Paul, slaves of Jesus Christ. The synergistic church demonstrates its commitment to God through praise and worship, prayer and fasting, and its focus on helping to fulfill the Great Commission.

The prophet Daniel understood the importance of being committed to God. Few people in history have been as influential as this prophet. Daniel rose from obscurity in Jerusalem to be the advisor and confidant of some of the greatest kings in the history of the world. In fact, Daniel's influence was so great that, at times, he even ruled over all of Babylon. How could this Israelite exile rise from tragedy to triumph? How could this slave become a trusted friend of the king? Daniel never let his position in life or the pressures around him change his commitments. Coupled with his faithfulness to God, his commitments enabled Daniel to become one of the greatest men of faith of the Old Testament.

The exiled nation of Israel faced many temptations in Babylon. It would be easy for them to forgo their commitment to God due to their circumstances. The temple of God in Jerusalem had been destroyed, thousands of men and women had been killed, and there was seemingly no hope left for Israel. Many believed that God had forsaken them. Because of this, many abandoned their faith and turned to pagan rituals. As slaves of the Babylonians, they left the laws of God and followed the gods of their captors. Daniel did not allow his circumstances to dictate his level of commitment to God. As advisor to Nebuchadnezzar, Belshazzar, Cyrus, and Darius, Daniel had many opportunities to reshuffle his priorities. His commitment to God often caused him to face death, but no matter the consequence, Daniel would not forsake the truths of his faith.

Daniel was committed to worshiping the true God of Israel and not chasing after idols. He was committed to maintaining his relationship with God through prayer and fasting. Daniel was also committed to advancing his faith and seeing people, even pagan kings, follow the one true God. These were priorities in Daniel's life. Underlying all of them was the understanding that God was sovereign. This trust in the power of God enabled Daniel to live a consecrated life.

WORSHIP AND PRAISE THAT LIFTS THE ROOF OFF

God explicitly told the children of Israel in the Law of Moses that He was the only true God. The Ten Commandments clearly indicated that Israel was to have no other gods before Him. Jehovah alone was to be worshiped. He gave them laws that governed the way He would relate to them and ways they could connect with Him. One way of worship was expressed through their eating practices. The Old Testament gave parameters on what God's people could and could not eat. This was an expression of their worship and allegiance to God. In addition to health reasons, many of the foods were banned because they were offered as sacrifices to pagan idols. Eating them would be worshiping gods other than Jehovah.

When Israel was defeated, Daniel and his friends were taken captive to the king's court. They were to be trained in the palace for service to the king. As part of their training, they were required to eat food from the king's table. This food was considered unclean in the Old Testament for it had most likely been sacrificed to idols. Daniel and his friends determined that they would not eat this food because their commitment to God would not allow them. The Bible says, "Daniel resolved not to defile himself with the royal food and wine, and he asked the chief official for permission not to defile himself" (Daniel 1:8). His captors could change a lot of things but not Daniel's heart.

This brought Daniel into conflict with the chief official responsible for him. The official assumed that without eating from the king's table, Daniel and his friends would suffer from malnutrition or disease. If Daniel and his friends looked sick from lack of eating, the officials would be punished. Daniel, however, trusted in an all-powerful God. He believed that if He was faithful to God's Word, God would be faithful to him.

He convinced the chief official to allow Shadrach, Meshach, Abednego, and himself to eat nothing but vegetables and water for ten days. At the end of this time, the young men looked healthier and better nourished than those who ate the royal food (Daniel 1:15). The official then allowed Daniel to keep the Law of God. Daniel fulfilled his commitment to glorify only God. As the young men grew and were faithful to God's Word, He gave them knowledge and understanding of all kinds of teaching and literature (Daniel 1:17). Their commitment resulted in blessing. Through a series of adventures and challenges, these exiles came to be some of the most powerful men in Babylon. Daniel became advisor to the king, and Shadrach, Meshach, and Abednego became governors of the province of Babylon, all because they were committed to God (Daniel 2:49).

The worship of God has been an integral part of how His people relate to Him. The Old Testament is filled with examples of God's people glorifying and honoring Him. From the early days of creation, Adam and his family built altars to God (Genesis 4:3,4). The Bible records songs of praise from Job, Moses, and many others (Job 1:20; Exodus 15:1–18). David, for example, wrote numerous majestic songs of adoration and praise to almighty God in heaven.

In the New Testament Church, worship was a vital part of life. Mary, the mother of Jesus, and Elizabeth, the mother of John the Baptist, both sang songs of praise to their God. Jesus also glorified His Father in heaven, modeling the way His followers should worship God. If anyone deserved to be worshiped on earth, it was He; but He lifted up the name of His Father God. In teaching the disciples about prayer, He began with the holiness of God (Matthew 6:19). Even the Holy Spirit came to glorify God (John 16:14).

Early Christians often went to the temple to pray and worship (Acts 3:1). They spent time together fellowshipping and praising God (Acts 2:46,47). Worship of the one true God separates God's people from the world around them. This worship is not only the necessary response to our loving Savior, but is also a message to the world about who God is. Our worship of Him expresses the elements of His character and attributes (Psalms 119 and 145), the power He has in the world (Psalm 47), the work He has done for us (Psalm 66), and the future we have when trusting in Him (Psalm 87). From these declarations of love to God, we reveal to the world how important it is that they also follow Christ.

The Impact of Praise and Worship on Today's Church

A revival of praise and worship has swept the church in the last few years. An emphasis on personal relationship and transformation has caused people to have a greater sense of connection with God and a greater desire to reverence and worship Him. While overall music sales have fallen recently, Christian music sales are up 9 percent. Praise and worship music makes up more than one-fifth of all Christian music sales.[1] Spiritual formation and devotional books are filling the shelves of Christian and secular bookstores. People desire to show their devotion and worship of God in tangible ways. They are redefining what it means to personally worship God. Just like Daniel, people are committed to honoring God through worship, and this worship is not confined to a Sunday service.

Dr. Elmer Towns, a leading historian of church growth, sees the emphasis on worship as indicative of the churches that are growing in this new decade. Through research, he has identified several methods that have been used in the last few years to reach our culture for Jesus Christ. The fastest growing churches in the 1970s were churches that emphasized bussing. In the 1980s, the "seeker-sensitive" model became the standard method for growing a church. In the 1990s, churches that emphasized small-group and cell ministries were attracting people. Towns now sees the churches that emphasize praise and worship music as the churches that will see the most growth. The church is turning its eyes on Christ and desires to worship Him.

The church of the twenty-first century is a church that has the roof off. The roof is off our churches because the praise of God has knocked it off its hinges. Interestingly enough, the term "worship service" is being used more and more to describe the times when God's people corporately gather together. In her book *Extravagant Worship*, Darlene Zschech, the worship leader of the Hillsongs Church in Sydney, Australia, said that true worship is extravagant worship. She defines extravagant worship as "worship that is beyond the limits...excessive, extremely abundant, over-generous, costly, precious and valuable."[2] As a church, we focus on our God in heaven and worship Him. Worship songs today are filled with personal references to God and each individual's relationship to Him. Some have explained the difference like this: in the past we sang about God, but today we are singing to God.

Worshiping God—Glorifying God in All We Do

In this renewal of worship, it is important to realize that our worship of God is not just confined to fifteen to thirty minutes of singing at the beginning of each service. True worship is more than listening to the current best-selling music CD. Our entire lives should be lived as an expression of true worship to God. Paul wrote in Romans 12:1, "I urge you, brethren, by the mercies of God, to present your bodies a living and holy sacrifice, acceptable to God, which is your spiritual service of worship." Paul was saying that our lives are a total expression of worship to God. We lay our lives on the altar and sacrifice who we are to acknowledge Him. When we obey God's commands and live righteously, we do it as an act of worship. This is the extravagant worship Darlene Zschech was talking about. True worship goes beyond the limits of song or time and pours into every aspect of life. Unlike previous decades of church growth techniques or distinctives, praise and worship is near and dear to the heart of God. This is more than a niche idea; it is the way God desires for us to live and move in His presence. As we glorify Him in all we do, we will find that He continues to conform us to the image of Christ.

The people who exalt the name of the Lord in song on Sunday but who do not live lives of holiness the rest of the week are not worshiping; they are just singing. We must engage our whole being—heart, mind, and soul—in our worship to God. We can praise God with our lips but not serve Him in our hearts. In the time of the prophet Joel, God's people acted like they were repenting. They had all the outward signs; but in their hearts, they did not mean what they were saying or doing. God rebuked them and said, "Tear your heart not your clothes to show repentance and worship" (Joel 2:13).

True worshipers, extravagant worshipers, are not concerned about form but about the object of their worship, the Lord Jesus Christ. In fact, true worship has little to do with style or music form. Many people are convinced that a certain style of music is why God is moving today. These people have missed the point. God inhabits the praises of His people, regardless of the style. He inhabits praise, not tempo. A theology of worship that glorifies only one worship style is a narrow view of Christ's inexhaustible riches.[3] If we limit our expression of faith to God by only our preferred means, we will never fully grasp the vastness of God's presence and work in our lives. It is often from others that we see and learn more about God.

True worship always results in synergy. If there is one thing

135

the Body of Christ should be able to agree upon, it is the worship of Jesus Christ. Churches and individuals who argue and fight about form and style in music and worship are spending more time in the works of the flesh than the works of the Spirit. To sing hallelujah to the Lord, it does not matter what our theological persuasion or distinctive doctrine, traditions, history, race, social status, or view of baptism. We need not argue about whether a form of expression is or is not worship. Everything we do in life should be done as an expression of love and adoration to our Savior and King. When we take the stories of what God has done in Scripture and in our lives and retell them to each other through art and music, we are glorifying God and testifying to others about who our God is. The beginning of synergy in a church or group of churches is always the worship of God. When we focus on Him, our differences become less and less significant. Let us take to heart the words of this hymn:

> Turn your eyes upon Jesus,
> look full in His wonderful face,
> and the things of earth will grow strangely dim,
> in the light of His glory and grace.[4]

As we grow closer together, may we look into His face and worship extravagantly.

PRAYER AND FASTING
KEEPS THE ROOF OFF

Not everyone loved Daniel's worship of God and God's subsequent blessing on him. While serving as advisor to King Darius, Daniel distinguished himself so much with his leadership skills that Darius desired to place him over the whole kingdom (Daniel 6:3). The other leaders were jealous of Daniel and tried to come up with ways to discredit him (v. 4), but Daniel lived such a holy life that they were unable to find any corruption in him. Daniel's integrity and fairness were known throughout the land. The only area of his life that they knew they could challenge was his commitment to the law of God (v. 5).

These men knew Daniel was committed to prayer. Three times a day, Daniel prayed and thanked God for all He had done for him. This worship and communication was a priority for Daniel. Every day, no matter what the circumstances, he would go to the upper room of his home where the windows opened to Jerusalem and would pray three times a day (v. 10). King Darius loved and respected Daniel, which caused the other leaders to hate him even more. These jealous leaders approached Darius to trick him into decreeing Daniel's death. Through flattery and manipulation, they convinced Darius to write a decree that for thirty days no one was to pray to any god or man except King Darius. The punishment for praying to another god would be death in the lion's den.

Daniel had a decision to make. He was the servant and advisor of the king and was soon to oversee the entire kingdom. The law did not require Daniel to pray to the king; he just could not pray to his God. Would Daniel follow the decree and not pray to God for thirty days? What would be most important for Daniel: personal advancement or commitment to God?

Daniel's priorities would not allow him to follow this decree because he was committed to prayer. When Daniel learned of the decree, he immediately went home to the upper room and prayed to his God (v. 10). He was a man of conviction, a man of priorities, and a leader. The law of the king was not as important as God's law.

Daniel's enemies were waiting for him. They saw him praying and immediately went to the king. When King Darius heard their report, he was greatly disturbed. In fact, he made every effort to save Daniel from the lion's den, but his law was binding. Daniel would be thrown into the lion's den and a stone placed over the entrance. The den was sealed so that no one could get in or out. Darius did not sleep all night as Daniel remained with the lions. At the first morning light, the king raced to the lion's den and called into the den, "Daniel, servant of the living God, has your God, whom you constantly serve, been able to deliver you from the lions?" (v. 20).

Daniel's voice answered from the black cave, "My God sent his angel and shut the lions' mouths, and they have not harmed me, inasmuch as I was found innocent before Him" (v. 22). God had saved Daniel! God had been with Daniel in the darkest and most dangerous of moments because Daniel had not compromised his commitment to prayer.

Like Daniel, we must be committed to prayer. Prayer and fasting were his strength in captivity. Christians who are called to live beyond the limits in this world must be plugged into God, the source of their strength. Prayer must saturate everything we do. It must permeate every new idea and old habit. It must be the first thing we do before beginning and the last before concluding. A church with no roof is a praying church.

Effective Prayer of the Synergistic Church

Many people pray, but the Bible tells us we must have effective prayer: "The effective prayer of a righteous man can accomplish much" (James 5:16). The Greek term for "effective" means "stretched-out prayer." The implication is not in length but in intensity. This is comparable to the athlete stretching for the finish line.

With the roof off our church, there is a constant connection to God. We should pray without ceasing (Luke 18:1; Matthew 7:7–11; 1 Thessalonians 5:15). In Luke 18:1, Jesus told His disciples "not to lose heart." Moreover, Jesus constantly reminded them never to cease praying. Those who search for God with all their hearts will find Him (Jeremiah 29:13). Jesus illustrated this kind of "effective" prayer in the Garden of Gethsemane.

138

Christ was in agony while praying *fervently* (Luke 22:44). The same word is used again to describe these kinds of prayers. Jesus was in agony, and His soul was "stretched out" to the point that His sweat became like drops of blood. The synergistic church must pray fervently, without ceasing or losing heart.

We need to understand that it is harder to pray than it is to preach the gospel. It is harder to intercede before God than it is to inspire others to serve God. We cannot fail in our commitment to prayer. If leaders are going to have the mighty anointing of the Holy Spirit upon their message and ministry, they will have to agonize in prayer before God. Prayer must begin with the leadership of the church. Sadly, too many churches and pastors depend on the prayers of a few retired ladies for spiritual renewal. It is not enough to have several people praying. The entire church, including the pastoral team, must be praying. The synergistic church will budget time and money into the week for prayer. Pastor Jim Cymbala of the Brooklyn Tabernacle has seen the power of a church built upon prayer. Brooklyn Tabernacle spends hours each week in prayer and fasting.

> Prayer must be the first thing we do before beginning and the last before concluding.

If you are the pastor of a local church, how important is prayer to you? Do you systematically plan for periods of prayer during the week? Many church staffs spend hours each week preparing the building for worship but do not prayerfully prepare their hearts for worship. Leonard Ravenhill summed up the issue well:

> No man is greater than his prayer life. The pastor who is not praying is playing; the people who are not praying are straying...We have many organizers, but few agonizers; many players and payers, few pray-ers; many singers, few clingers; lots of pastors, few wrestlers; many fears, few

tears; much fashion, little passion; many interferers, few intercessors; many writers, but few fighters. Failing here, we fail everywhere.[5]

If we are ever to see a real revival of God's Spirit in our churches, if we are ever to live in synergy with His will and power, we must be praying churches.

This commitment to prayer is necessary for the growth of the church. Before we can advance into the marketplace of ministry (where the church walls are down), the roof must be off in preparation.

A praying church undergoes *spiritual conditioning.* The spiritual muscles of the pastor and people grow as they "stretch" and "work" them out through supplication before God. The quality of our quiet time will result in either spiritual strength or spiritual weakness. Many pastors are failing in ministry because they are busy preparing messages or developing programs rather than praying for people. It is hypocritical to preach to people before first praying for them. The source of our strength is our connection to God. Without this conditioning, we will not be able to finish the course.

A praying church is being *spiritually cleaned.*[6] The journey of leadership consists of dirty, muddy roads. Each day the soul of the minister is soiled by the world. We will make mistakes as we move past the limitations that come against us. If we are not careful, the grime of life will create non-Christian attitudes in the heart, and sin can be committed—even in the ministry. Thus, the prayer life becomes a time of spiritually washing the heart, mind, emotion, and will before God. The more time the leader spends each day in prayer, the more adjustments will be made in attitudes and actions in ministry.

Every great revival has been characterized by confession of sin to God and one another. Revival also comes when confession replaces criticism. There is constant temptation in the ministry to criticize fellow ministers. The humble servant leader is careful to listen and understand before commenting about various issues and individuals in the church.

A praying church acknowledges it is in *spiritual conflict.* The evangelist and pastor are in a spiritual war for the souls of men and women. We must all realize that we wrestle not against flesh and blood but against principalities and powers of the air. The most effective way to fight the enemies of God is on our knees in prayer. When the time of prayer is neglected, the battle is left unfought. How many victories have been won by the hordes of hell because God's people never entered the field of battle? How many battles have been lost because the Church of God never bowed its knees in prayer? When we neglect prayer, we are weakening our defense before Satan and his kingdom.

Fasting Demonstrates Dependence

The committed Christian must be committed to prayer and fasting. I (Bill) believe that fasting is the only spiritual discipline that meets the requirements of 2 Chronicles 7:14: "If my people, who are called by my name, will humble themselves and pray and seek my face and turn from their wicked ways, then will I hear from heaven and will forgive their sin and will heal their land" (NIV). In 1994, God spoke to my heart to fast for forty days. During that time, He revealed to me the need for a book on fasting. In that book, *The Coming Revival,* I identified several benefits of fasting and prayer:

- It is a biblical way to truly humble oneself in the sight of God (Psalm 35:13; Ezra 8:21).

- It brings revelation by the Holy Spirit of a person's true spiritual condition, resulting in brokenness, repentance, and change.

- It is a crucial means for personal revival because it brings the inner workings of the Holy Spirit into play in a most unusual, powerful way.

- It helps us better understand the Word of God by making it more meaningful, vital, and practical.
- It transforms prayer into a richer and more personal experience.
- It can result in dynamic personal revival—being controlled and led by the Spirit and regaining a strong sense of spiritual determination.
- It can restore the loss of one's first love for our Lord.[7]

Elmer Towns points out that in fasting, we are not manipulating God but obeying His commands.[8] Fasting is not an end in itself but a means by which we can practice humility before God. In fasting, more than any other discipline, we are denying ourselves so that we might be filled with God. By humbling our souls, fasting reduces the power of self so that the Spirit can do a more intense work within us. As a result, He can accomplish His will in us and do even more than we can ask or imagine.

Campus Crusade for Christ began in 1951 with a 24-hour prayer chain on the campus of UCLA. As people prayed, we began to see a move of God on that campus. Hundreds of young people, many of whom later became leaders in their countries, were touched by the power of God. This was a direct result of the prayer and fasting of those committed to seeking God's will for the ministry of Campus Crusade for Christ.

The synergistic church must be a fasting church. We strongly recommend the book *Fasting Can Change Your Life*, by Drs. Jerry Falwell and Elmer Towns. This book is a collection of insights on fasting and the local church from pastors and church leaders such as D. James Kennedy, Dutch Sheets, Jack Hayford, and others. There are chapters on leading the church through forty-day fasts, fasting for miracles, how to teach fasting, and several other relevant topics for the church that wants to reemphasize fasting and prayer. It shows the need for personal and corporate times of prayer and fasting.

This often means the leadership of the church should call the church to fasting. There were definite times in the Bible when God's people were corporately called to fast. When doing this, it is necessary to teach and preach on fasting for several weeks to prepare the people.[9] It is very important to be led by God during these times, along with using God-given common sense. It is unrealistic to attempt a forty-day fast if a person has never fasted before. Begin with a one-day fast and follow the instructions from the Bible and other helps that are available. Those with medical conditions who cannot fast entire meals should never feel guilty or "less spiritual." They should consult a physician on what they can do. Perhaps they could fast from a certain food, or abstain from a particular activity.

I (Bill) have continued to undergo a forty-day fast for national and world revival every year since God laid it upon my heart in 1994. The results in my personal life and ministry have been dramatic. I am so committed to the priority of fasting and prayer that I dedicated the $1 million Templeton prize I received in 1996 to the distribution of fasting and prayer materials in many languages worldwide.

It is so important to seek God's face through fasting and prayer. The leader must be connected to God through prayer. It is impossible to overexaggerate the importance of prayer. Jesus said, "If you ask Me anything in My name, I will do it" (John 14:14). It is absolutely necessary to keep this line of communication with God open so that the roof of the church stays off.

EVANGELISM FLOURISHES WHEN THE ROOF IS OFF

Daniel was committed to more than just prayer and worship. He was committed to sharing God with his captors. It is interesting to note that Daniel influenced the key leaders of his day.

By his testimony and faithfulness, he led King Nebuchadnezzar to acknowledge Jehovah as the most high God (Daniel 4:2,3). Later in his life, Nebuchadnezzar declared Daniel's God as the majestic King of Heaven (Daniel 4:34–37). When Daniel's enemies tried to slander him, his testimony was so strong that they could find no area in which to accuse him. They therefore determined to accuse him regarding his commitment to God. As Daniel was being thrown into the pit, King Darius said to him, "Your God whom you constantly serve will Himself deliver you" (Daniel 6:16). Daniel's priorities led to a powerful testimony. He served God continually, even in the face of death. God delivered Daniel, and King Darius had Daniel's enemies thrown to the lions. Because of the testimony of Daniel, King Darius issued a new law protecting Israelite exiles from persecution when they served God. Darius also decreed that all the men of his kingdom should fear and reverence the God of Daniel. Daniel's commitment to his priorities allowed him to have a powerful testimony before the king and before all of Babylon.

Evangelism Creates Synergy Through Reconciliation

What is the meaning of the term "evangelism"? The Lausanne Covenant of the International Congress on World Evangelism (1974) provides a comprehensive definition:

> To evangelize is to spread the good news that Jesus Christ died for our sins and was raised from the dead according to the Scriptures, and that as the reigning Lord, He now offers the forgiveness of sins and the liberating gifts of the Spirit to all who repent and believe. Our Christian presence in the world is indispensable to evangelism, and so is that kind of dialogue whose purpose is to listen sensitively in order to understand. But evangelism itself is the proclamation of the historical, biblical Christ as Savior

and Lord, with a view to persuading people to come to Him personally and so be reconciled to God. In issuing the gospel invitation, we have no liberty to conceal the cost of discipleship. Jesus still calls all who would follow Him to deny themselves, take up their cross, and identify themselves with His new community. The results of evangelism include obedience to Christ, incorporation into His Church and responsible service in the world.[10]

World evangelism is the supreme goal of the Church. Evangelism is to bear witness to the gospel with the soul aflame and to teach and preach with the express purpose of making disciples of those who hear.[11] Even though Christ has commissioned every Christian to participate in world evangelization (Matthew 28:19), the leader must be focused on the cause of evangelism.

In the last one hundred years, the Church has witnessed positive movement on this front. Virtually every branch of the Christian church is being blessed with growth through evangelism. According to one estimate, the Pentecostal movement—which had its humble beginnings in Topeka, Kansas, and Azusa Street in Los Angeles, California, in the early 1900s—now numbers over 533 million people.[12] The same study estimates that by 2025, Pentecostals/Charismatics will reach 1 billion in number. Evangelicals are also seeing God at work with worldwide membership now reaching over 200 million people. The rate of annual growth is especially encouraging among all Protestant groups. Another study estimates that Pentecostals/Charismatics are growing at a rate of 7.4 percent, while evangelicals are growing at a rate of 5.7 percent worldwide.[13]

Despite these encouraging figures, it is estimated that unreached people groups still number as high as 1 billion people! Unquestionably, leaders must continue to be passionate about bringing men and women to Jesus Christ, taking seriously Christ's command to "go into all the world and preach the gospel to all creation" (Mark 16:15).

The fundamental mission of Jesus Christ was to seek and save that which was lost (Luke 19:10). Christ died on the cross in order that He might draw all men to Himself (John 12:32). Paul calls Christ's work at Calvary "reconciliation" (2 Corinthians 5). He then tells us that we, as Christ's ambassadors, have been given the ministry of reconciliation (v. 5). What does it mean to have a ministry of reconciliation, and what is the message of reconciliation? Paul writes that reconciliation is the work of Christ drawing men and women to Himself:

> Remember that you were at that time separate from Christ, excluded from the commonwealth of Israel, and strangers to the covenants of promise, having no hope and without God in the world. But now, in Christ Jesus you who formerly were far off have been brought near by the blood of Christ (Ephesians 2:12–14).

The Bible contains God's plan for reconciliation and understanding. Some scholars believe that this word, reconciliation, is the ultimate message of all of God's work in the Bible—the restoration of a right covenant fellowship with God. Reconciliation means the bringing together of things that are apart. The Bible's opening picture portrays humanity separating from its Creator and God working to reconcile this divide. From that first break in communion with God, God's plan for reconciliation unfolds in Scripture and climaxes in the work of the cross.

The great paradox of Christian ministry is that we who were unable to reconcile ourselves to God are given the ministry of reconciliation. The goal of the Great Commission is not to establish an institutional church or denomination, but to share the gospel and make disciples of all men. We are not so bold as to think that we as individuals can save others, but we can initiate their reconciliation by pointing them to Jesus Christ. Jesus Christ is the center of our faith and the center of our message.

Since we fear the Lord, we try to persuade men...

Christ's love compels us because One died for all, therefore all died; and He died for all that those who live should no longer live for themselves but for Him who died for them and was raised again. So now we regard no one from a worldly point of view (2 Corinthians 5:11,14).

We must persuade men to embrace the Savior who died for them. We must challenge sinners and give them opportunity to accept the risen Savior. Through this message of reconciliation, Christ has torn down the walls between God and man. This is the passion of the leader. We must be sensitive to the needs of the seekers as we point them to Christ, but we must also be Savior-sensitive, not neglecting our message: Jesus Christ, reconciler of the world.

Connecting to the Culture

The Church must connect to the culture around it in three ways to be effective in the world in which we now live. These adaptations will enable the church with no roof to knock down the walls that have hindered the evangelism of the world.

First, we cannot debate minutia but must focus on essentials. A post-Christian world wants to know if there is a God and how He can be experienced. They are not concerned with the debated details of Christianity because they have not bought into the big picture yet. Arguments over Calvinism and Arminianism, the Eucharist, or modes of baptism are irrelevant when people do not know if God exists. By focusing on the essentials of the Christian faith (there is a God, man is a sinner, and Christ died to allow a relationship with God), we can help the world come to know Christ. We must not allow denominational trappings to limit the ability of anyone to receive and follow Christ.

Second, we cannot condemn those who reject our Lord but must reason with them in winsome gentleness, love, and respect. The greatest sign of desperation in any argument of debate is to fall to personal attack. For centuries, Christians have fallen into the trap of name-calling. Rather than reaching out in love, we have attacked those who did not immediately embrace Christ. We must tone down our verbiage and strengthen our love so that we might better lead them to Christ. McClaren points out that it was easy to dismiss Buddhists and Muslims when they lived on the other side of the world, but the reality is that they now live next door to us. They will know we are Christians by our love, not by the volume of our speech. We must find ways to interact with those around us who do not follow Christ. We do not compromise our message or our passion, but we must model the love and humility Christ practiced on earth. Remember, Christ's harshest words were not for the pagans of His day but for the self-righteous Pharisees who treated others with contempt. It is a very important fact learned from many surveys and years of experience that Jesus is usually respected and admired even by non-Christians while His followers are often held in low esteem. Why? Because we fail to obey His teachings and follow His example.

The last component in reaching our culture is patience. We must not rush people but help them come to Christ at a healthy pace. We are programmed for a major conversion event or an instant salvation experience. However, the history of Christianity has been more process-centered than event-centered. Conversion for many people is a long process of commitment and understanding. Too many people have been rushed to commit to Christ before they have fully accepted the message of the gospel and are ready to repent and fully commit to the life of faith. As a result, they have abandoned their faith. In this new period in history, we must enable people to understand what they are committing to as the Holy Spirit works in them.

148

Becoming Purposeful in Our Witness

The greatest mode of evangelism in the world today is still personal evangelism. Every member of the Body of Christ, from leadership to laity, is to be a personal witness who takes the initiative to share the most joyful news ever announced about our Lord Jesus Christ. Leaders do not just train others for evangelism; they do evangelism. They are personal witnesses for Jesus Christ. The greatest thing any follower of Jesus Christ can do is win someone to Jesus Christ.

Witnesses are those whose life and words are Christlike. They demonstrate that Christ is in control of their life. The Holy Spirit came to glorify Christ and to bear witness to Him; therefore, Spirit-directed Christians will glorify Christ and tell others about Him. They will help fulfill the Great Commission given by our Lord Jesus Christ before He ascended into heaven (Matthew 28:19,20).

People express themselves to the world around them through actions and words. This communicates to others who we are and what we believe. To have an impact on other people, our words and actions cannot be in conflict. Our walk must be consistent with our message. If we tell others about the love and lordship of Christ yet they see actions that do not reflect His love or lordship in our lives, we communicate a contradictory message to them. Carnal Christians communicate disturbing and confusing messages to others. If we are not totally surrendered to Christ and His lordship in our lives, we can destroy our witness to people and hinder the work of God in their lives. Passionate leaders guard their actions and monitor their words.

Many people feel inadequate when it comes to personally sharing their faith. Many ministers can comfortably explain Christ's message to thousands at a time but struggle telling an individual the plan of salvation. Many have the passion for evangelism but do not know how to personally evangelize. This problem results from several causes. It may be a reliance on self and a lack of reliance on the Holy Spirit. Remember, Jesus told His disciples not to go witnessing until they received the infilling of the Holy Spirit. He knew that human ability alone was inadequate for the spiritual task of evangelism. We need to make sure we have appropriated the fullness of the Holy Spirit, confessed any known sin in our lives, received forgiveness and cleansing in accordance with 1 John 1:9, and expressed our reliance on Him. This will inject a new spiritual power into our witnessing.

The sense of inadequacy in personal witnessing could stem from fear or a lack of boldness. This can also be overcome by the Holy Spirit. God has not given us a spirit of fear but of power, love, and a sound mind (2 Timothy 1:7). Our love for God cannot help but overflow in our witness to others. The individual who struggles in this area should consult my (Bill) Gold Medallion–winning book, *Witnessing Without Fear*, where these issues are discussed at length. The leader must overcome the fear factor in witnessing through prayer and practice.

CONCLUSION

Our faithfulness in our commitment to God keeps the roof off the synergistic church. When the roof is off, we will wholeheartedly praise and worship our Creator God. Through prayer and fasting, we keep our connection to God open through earnest conversation with Him. This commitment to listening and speaking to God is what keeps the roof off. When we are committed to following the Lord, God knocks down the walls that would limit us in reaching out to others. Just like the children of Israel outside the fortified city of Jericho, God will use our shout of praise to knock the walls down, enabling us to evangelize the world. In the synergistic church, the roof is blown off with praise and the walls are brought down by our desire to introduce others to Christ.

PART TWO

A Church with No Walls

CHAPTER 7

Interdependent Cooperation

L ook around," Jeff Evans said to Erik Weihenmayer. "Just take a second and look around." His words were simple; there was nothing special about them unless you understand the context in which they were said. Erik Weihenmayer is blind, completely blind; and the two men were standing on top of the world, Mount Everest.[1] On May 24, 2001, Erik and his team of 19 climbed 29,035 feet to reach the summit of the world's tallest mountain. Only a few brave explorers have accomplished this incredible feat, none of them blind. Almost 90 percent of all climbers fail to reach the summit; many fail to return home.

After several months of climbing treacherous ice fields, fighting bitter cold and wind shear of over 100 miles per hour, Erik Weihenmayer became the first blind man to conquer Everest, achieving the seemingly impossible. This Herculean achievement has caused people to compare Erik to Helen Keller. How did a blind man from Colorado make it to the top? The answer is simple: teamwork. Mountain climber Pasquale Scaturro assembled a team of climbers that helped Erik reach the summit. Erik was an accomplished climber who had already climbed Mount Kilimanjaro in Africa, but Everest would be a greater challenge. Across ridges with 10,000-foot vertical falls on either side, Erik followed the sound of a bell fastened to the back of the team member in front of him. He listened to his fellow climbers' verbal directions and trusted them to lead him to safety. He walked across ladder bridges that spanned chasms hundreds of feet deep. He fought snowstorms and temperatures 30 degrees below zero while wearing oxygen tanks to breathe.

Many wondered how Erik would contribute to the expedition. Would he put people at risk and slow down the expedition? Apparently not. Eric Alexander, a fellow climber, called Erik the "heart and soul of the team . . . He won't let you quit." Although Erik was an experienced climber, he needed Alexander, Scaturro, Evans, and the others to make it to the top. It takes the whole team to climb Everest. These men became the eyes for Erik as he climbed. He became their heart. They enabled him to do the impossible because they were a team, but they needed Erik as well. He kept them motivated to keep going as they helped him make his way. He would not let them quit!

The partnership these men formed over the months of climbing is incredible. How many times did Erik entrust his life to those around him? How many times did they entrust their lives to Erik? It took each of them working together to make it to the top. It took a team to accomplish the goal. It was a team that was greater as a whole than any individual person alone—a team built on synergy.

NO CHURCH IS AN ISLAND

The days of ministry in isolation are over. The church must form strong, viable partnerships if it is to make an impact in the twenty-first century. We must work together with those around us if we are to make a difference for the gospel. While it has been sufficient in the past to create individual churches or ministries, the new age of ministry requires collaboration. Those called to lead the church must unite with other leaders to accomplish the task. It will take all of God's people working together.

Many churches have thrived in this isolation. Like little islands of refuge in their community, these churches rise up from an ocean of evil around them. Long distances of philosophy and theology separate some churches from each other. Those who choose to interact with these different islands (churches) are forced to use great effort. Many are happy as long as their island is growing, and are supportive of others as long as it does not require extended effort. Some churches are not even separated by beliefs; they simply have not taken the time to work together with other churches around them. The church beyond the limits must unite with those around it to form a strong force to reach the community.

Models for strong leadership have often been built around strong, magnetic personalities. People like Henry Ford, Andrew Carnegie, Aimee Simple McPherson, and D. L. Moody are considered examples of successful leadership. They were rugged individualists who attracted followings and achieved great results. They were the great leaders of their day. Their legacy is felt even today.

The Bible's picture of effective ministry and leadership is built around the concept of Holy Spirit–inspired teamwork and partnership. Jesus selected the twelve disciples, the early Christians chose seven deacons, and Paul chose partners for his missionary journeys. Just like these early Christians, we must realize that it will take strategic partnerships of mutual respect and admiration to achieve the leadership task we are called to accomplish. Just like Erik Weihenmayer, we will need a team to help us reach the summit.

This truth is reflected even in corporate America. In recent years, the importance of teamwork and cooperation has risen to the forefront in the leadership culture. Old paradigms are collapsing, and people now see the value of teamwork. Businesses and organizations are realizing that old, antiquated forms of authority are not working. People today are interested in words like synergy, networking, sharing, and community. "Hierarchy is out—it slows everything down," says Betsy Morris of *Fortune* magazine. "The conventional desk job is out . . . Employees think of themselves as knowledge workers—their office is the information they carry with them . . . A CEO on a pedestal is definitely out; a CEO as a platoon servant leader is in."[2]

Paul, the Model for Ministry Partnership

The apostle Paul understood the necessity of ministry partnerships. His ministry was filled with examples of teamwork. Relationships were vital to Paul. To accomplish his mission in life, Paul needed fellow workers such as Luke, Timothy, Barnabas, John Mark, Titus, and others. Each of these individuals collaborated to create a more effective team. However, Paul was careful; he did not align himself with everyone. In fact, he often warned against collaborating with those who would shipwreck the faith (1 Timothy 1:18,19). Even though Paul knew there were dangers, he realized that it would take everyone in the Body of Christ, each doing his or her part, to fulfill the Great Commission. Just like Paul, we also need to work together to accomplish the work of God.

Paul and Barnabas: Partners in Ministry

Paul and Barnabas were one of the first missionary teams. After Paul's conversion experience on the road to Damascus, it was Barnabas who brought him to the elders in Jerusalem. Barnabas's name means "son of encouragement," and he lived up to his name in Paul's life.

Barnabas went to Antioch to investigate a report that many were coming to the Lord (Acts 11:21,22). Upon arriving, Barnabas, full of the Holy Spirit, saw God's hand at work and knew that Antioch needed someone to help them in their journey of faith. He sought out Paul, and for a year they ministered together in Antioch (Acts 11:25,26). Together they formed a powerful ministry partnership. They understood that their effectiveness was doubled through teamwork, and together they launched a missionary crusade that brought the gospel to all of Galatia. The Antioch church sent Paul and Barnabas to evangelize the region. The Holy Spirit instituted this ministry team: "Set apart for Me Barnabas and Saul for the work to which I have called them" (Acts 13:2). God Himself had brought Paul and Barnabas together. Today, God divinely directs certain organizations and groups to join together. He sets apart groups that will work together for the task to which He calls them.

At Iconium and Lystra, Paul and Barnabas faced death together (Acts 14:5,19). On the island of Cyprus, they saw a Roman proconsul come to Christ (Acts 13:12), and in Antioch Pisidia, a great many believed (Acts 13:48). They appointed church leaders where they established churches; and upon returning to Antioch, they reported all that God had done (Acts 14:23,27). Together they achieved more than they could have done alone. Their partnership provided both accountability and fellowship as they ministered for God. It is God's plan for His ministers to cooperate in ministry and evangelism. Paul did not face death alone at Lystra; the Holy Spirit provided Barnabas to encourage him. Barnabas did not have to evangelize Cyprus alone; the Holy Spirit provided Paul to help him. As God directs us, we must cooperate with other leaders to form ministry teams that provide fellowship and accountability as we work for God.

Paul and Silas: Partners Through Adversity

In later missionary journeys, Paul traveled with Silas because he and John Mark had a disagreement (Acts 15:39). Even in God-ordained partnerships, disagreements can arise. The disagreement was later resolved between Paul and John Mark (2 Timothy 4:11), so the division did not stop the ministry of Christ. They separated and continued to minister the gospel. Barnabas and John Mark returned to Cyprus, and Paul took Silas into Syria and Cilicia.

Soon after, a young disciple named Timothy joined Paul and Silas (Acts 16:1). These men traveled to Philippi preaching and teaching the gospel. Here we see the relationship of Paul and Silas being tested. Among other miracles they performed, the apostles cast an evil spirit out of a fortune-telling slave (Acts 16:16–24). Upon finding that their livelihood was gone, the girl's owners seized Paul and Silas and cast them into prison where they were flogged and then chained inside the prison overnight.

It is the responsibility of leaders to pour themselves into the generation that follows.

Despite their pain and humiliation, Paul and Silas trusted in God and in each other and began to sing and worship while bound in chains. As they praised the Lord, God sent an earthquake that opened the doors of the jail and broke the chains that bound them (Acts 16:26). How could Paul and Silas, bruised and bleeding, worship God and see past this trial? It was a direct result of their view of God and their partnership. Leaders need each other in order to stay focused during adversity. Synergy creates shared strength that enables a team to stand in the face of difficulty. Paul and Silas drew strength from each other to persevere in the face of danger. Trials and tribulations will come in ministry; but by forming strong partnerships, we can better face adversity. "Iron sharpens iron, so one man sharpens another" (Proverbs 27:17). By joining with others, we can increase our effectiveness, especially when we confront the struggles of life.

We wish we could say that you will never face adversity or trials. The reality is that we all face trials, and at times many find themselves in chains at midnight. However, we can still worship God by faith, even in the darkest hour. This can be done by surrounding ourselves with fellow leaders who help keep us focused and on target. We can hold each other mutually accountable and lift each other up in various ways. We can then watch the chains fall off together as we worship through the trials and fight the attacks of Satan through the enabling power of the Holy Spirit.

Paul and Timothy: Partners for the Future

Timothy proved to be a great friend to Paul. From Paul's two letters to this young minister of the gospel, it is clear that he deeply loved Timothy, calling him his "true child in the faith" (1 Timothy 1:2). Timothy also respected and listened to Paul, even following his direction regarding circumcision (Acts 16:3). Their partnership was that of mentor and student. Paul knew that every successful leader must have a successor. Just as Jesus mentored the disciples, Elijah mentored Elisha, and Moses mentored Joshua, Paul helped young Timothy become a leader. Paul's understanding of ministry allowed him to see past his own life. Synergy is not only for the present but also for the future.

Paul encouraged Timothy to serve as an elder despite his young age (1 Timothy 4:12). He also instructed Timothy in the essential doctrines to which the church should adhere (1 and 2 Timothy). It is apparent from Paul's writings that Timothy was an important part of his life. He understood that it is the responsibility of leaders to pour themselves into the generation that follows in order that they might continue the work of God when they are gone. Just as Paul partnered with Timothy for the future, every leader should be mentoring someone for the future. Leaders who invest themselves in the lives of younger leaders create a legacy that will survive long past their lifetimes.

Paul and Demas: The Dangers of Partnerships

Demas was a fellow worker with Paul. While imprisoned in Rome, Paul wrote letters to the church at Colosse and to Philemon who was a part of that church. In both letters, Paul sent greetings from his coworker, Demas, who was with him. Very little is known about Demas other than these passages. He apparently followed Paul and Luke into the Roman prison, yet something happened between the writing of Colossians and the writing of Paul's second letter to Timothy. During this time, Paul learned that partnerships sometimes break your heart.

Exactly what happened we do not know since Paul did not give us the details. "Make every effort to come to me soon; for Demas, having loved this present world, has deserted me and gone to Thessalonica" (2 Timothy 4:9,10). In the darkness of a Roman dungeon and dependent upon the help of friends for nourishment and protection, Paul found himself deserted by his fellow worker, Demas. His only explanation was that Demas loved this world.

Partnerships can be dangerous. The interdependence we achieve by relying upon another makes us vulnerable if one party deserts the other. Paul was alone. He learned firsthand what it was like to be left in the time of need. What is interesting is that Paul does not condemn Demas or complain about the problem. He simply acknowledges that Demas is gone and tells why. Demas had fallen victim to worldliness. Perhaps the dungeon and adversity were too much for him or the temptations of the world overpowered him. Followers of Christ are not to love the world because everything in the world does not come from the

Father (1 John 2:15–17). Demas could not see past his present world and see the potential world like Paul did. While Paul fixed his mind on things above, Demas could not see past the darkness of the Roman dungeon. Demas saw the present defeat; Paul saw the potential victory.

Paul and Demas's partnership did not work out as planned. Demas defected, and Paul was alone. However, this did not sour Paul on relationships and partnering in ministry. In the same passage in which he announces Demas's defection, Paul calls for Timothy and John Mark to join him (2 Timothy 4:11). Remember, it was John Mark with whom Paul had problems earlier in his ministry. Paul was willing to mend fences and continue to partner with others because he still saw the potential of working together. Even though his present situation was marked by Demas's leaving, Paul saw the potential of cooperation based upon synergy. We must expect dangers and even heartbreak when we work with others, but the reward of synergistic ministry is far greater than the danger.

BUILDING BRIDGES TO CREATE SYNERGY

People separate themselves politically, socially, racially, and economically. This same separation has also worked its way into the Body of Christ. Many Christians live isolated from each other, never working together. Even worse, they are often competing against one another. Even though human beings are made for fellowship and community, we build walls between each other and portray fellow Christians in a bad light because of pride and ignorance. We are at our best when we are connected with others; we are at our worst when we selfishly compete.

Despite technology's advancements in travel and communication, we still alienate ourselves from others. While information is at an all-time high, compassion remains at an all-time low. We have developed marvelous new means of communication which have enabled us to yell louder and more quickly at each other than ever before; but for all his ingenuity, Bill Gates cannot teach us to love each other.

Paul writes that we have been given the ministry of reconciliation (2 Corinthians 5:18). This ministry involves taking the message of reconciliation—that Christ is drawing men and women to Himself through the cross—to a world in need of His love and forgiveness. Paul also says that reconciliation is the bringing together of different groups of people (Ephesians 2:14–16). The ministry of reconciliation is the work of God's people to build bridges between people and Christ and between each other. As leaders concerned about effective ministry, we are called to be bridge builders.

Randy Jumper, a young evangelist who has served with me (James) for years, spoke at a gathering of church leaders about the necessity of building bridges. He not only serves as an evangelist but has made an enormous contribution to the development of this book. We recommend that every pastor prayerfully consider using his ministry in their local church. During his message he emphasized:

> The ministry of reconciliation in one sense is bridge building. People are separated, and we are called to unite them to God and to each other. Leaders are called to bridge the divide of stereotypes, unbelief, and lack of faith. The bridges we will be called to build will be different for each of us. We each have a unique calling, but there are certain bridges we are called to build. They leap from the pages of Scripture and the context of life. Christ has torn down the walls that separate us. The rubble is at our feet. What will we do with the stones in front of us? Will we build more walls, or will we build bridges? [3]

If we want to build synergistic church communities, we

must begin to build bridges toward each other. Christ has torn down the walls of separation (Ephesians 2:14). We must now build bridges that allow us to partner together. It will require effort and sacrifice on our part, but we must work together. Whatever the ministry in which we are involved, we must make it a priority to connect with others around us. As Christ has reconciled the lost to Himself, we must mirror that same Christlike quality to the world as we work together.

THE PATHWAYS OF COOPERATION: SYNERGY BEGINS IN THE LOCAL CHURCH

The local church is the first place the principles of synergy and cooperation need to be present. It would be discouraging to learn how many people have been turned away from the gospel because the church to which they were exposed was filled with backstabbing and politics. How sad it must make Christ to see His Church filled with division and mistrust. When the local church cannot function due to a lack of cooperation, how do we expect the global Church to make an impact for Christ and for the glory of the Father?

To create synergy in the local church, each member must realize the value of cooperation. This begins with valuing the people in the church. Everybody is a somebody in the Body of Christ. When we view each other as fellow members of Christ's Body, we will treat each other as such. This means that pastors will view themselves as Christ's servants to laity, and not manipulate them or view them as less important to God. The members of the local church all contribute vital spiritual gifts that make a healthy church grow (Ephesians 4:16). When members do not do their part by utilizing their gifts, or they neglect the gifts of others, the church will never achieve all God has for it.

Whether we realize it or not, it is imperative for the local church to grow together internally before expanding outward.

Healthy churches are not just growing in number; they are also growing in strength. A tree with many branches and no roots or a thin trunk will not support its own weight. This interdependence and synergy will create new avenues of ministry as we unite. Just like Paul and Silas, we will call upon each other in the night to help us to stand strong. There will be times when it will be necessary to rely upon the strength of others because our strength is gone. The church that is interdependent can do this.

Building Bridges Across the Generational Divide

As synergistic church leaders, we must build a bridge that connects the various generations. As the prophet Joel explains, God is seeking to work through old and young alike:

> It will come about after this that I will pour out My Spirit on all mankind; and your *sons and daughters* will prophesy, your *old men* will dream dreams, your *young men* will see visions (Joel 2:28, emphasis added).

A trend is developing in our churches and in our ministerial ranks that is alarming. It is the disenfranchisement between the younger generation of the church and the older generation. The greatest point of conflict is in worship styles, particularly music. The older generation feels threatened because what they have created seems to be slipping away due to a lack of respect. The younger generation feels threatened because their opinions and perspectives seem irrelevant to their leaders. The younger generation sees no value in the old ways, and the older generation sees no need for newer methods. This same disparity is found even among church leadership. In most cases, both groups are committed to the same beliefs and convictions; they just express them differently. They remain fragmented because they would rather separate and blame than communicate and love. This is a direct result of the cultural shift that is taking place in the world.

As discussed in Chapter 1, the information divide is rapidly changing the landscape of the world and thus the church. We must not fall victim to its results.

What if Paul had not discipled Timothy? What if Timothy had dismissed Paul as antiquated and useless? Where would the early church have been if these men had ignored the leading of God? We cannot allow cultural bias and personal dislike to infect the church. We must bridge this divide if we are to see Joel 2 become a reality in our churches.

How can we bridge this gap? It will come with work and cooperation. It will take trust and time. It means that the younger generation must get past their suspicions of institutions and participate in the church structure. It means they cannot demand change overnight. They must learn to respect and understand the heritage of their faith. Why? Because even though they love independence, we need each other to accomplish the Great Commission.

The information divide is rapidly changing the landscape of the world and thus the church.

In return, older leaders must meet them in the middle. They must understand the need for change and the updating of methods, and must look to youth for counsel and advice. They cannot look down upon new ideas, because their ideas were new once also. They must mentor and guide young Timothys to see past their suspicions so the younger can benefit from the experience of the older. The older generation needs to seek input from the younger generation, allowing them to become the eyes and ears of the culture around them. They need to prepare the younger generation for the day, should Jesus tarry, when they will be the older generation. Do not allow choice in music or service style to become barriers to cooperation. Unite to advance the kingdom of God.

Building Bridges Across the Racial Divide

Campus Crusade for Christ has always sought to bring the message of Christ to all people. On many occasions, we have been privileged to work side by side with ethnic groups as we help evangelize the world. In 1981, we sponsored "Chicago '81," a conference of over 1,500 leaders and laymen to help influence African-Americans for Christ. From that conference was born Destiny Movement, Inc., a ministry of African-Americans to African-Americans. It was supported almost entirely by contributions from the staff of Campus Crusade for Christ. It became a priority for us to work together with ethnic leaders in reaching the world. This is God's plan for world evangelization. Since these meetings, this ministry has grown and expanded with great blessing.

The melting pot of America is turning into a mosaic of many different cultures and groups. In a postmodern world, diversity is celebrated and, in a sense, better resembles where the church should be. The value of different ethnicities and heritages is not a threat to Christianity. Creativity and variety are characteristics of the world that God created, and He saw that it was very good. The leader must recognize this and create ways to partner with those of different ethnicities. It will take healing and restoration between races that have been separated for years. The bridge of love and compassion must be built. It is the will of the Father.

The result of reconciliation (our bridge building) is the picture of true community—a community in Christ where there is no Greek and no Jew, no circumcision or uncircumcision, no slave or free, no male or female, no rich or poor, no white or black; just Jesus Christ as the all in all. We cannot ignore the years of sinful racial separation and profiling that have existed in the church. In your community, it may be necessary to join with others in confession of these sins and restoration of destroyed relationships, but do not allow this effort to consist merely of superficial marches and "reconciliation lunches." It is time that the Church of Jesus Christ take the lead in combating the sins of racism that infect our communities. Partner with other churches to reach your community through joint outreaches and service projects. One of the easiest ways to do this is to join together in worship and missions. Combine services with other churches in your town and sit together. Model to the children the importance of worshiping together with different ethnic groups. In your church, do not be afraid to have staffs that are ethnically diverse. Encourage people to grow past racial bias in the community by allowing them to use the leadership gifts God has given them. In your own church and community, build bridges across the racial divide.

THE ART OF PARTNERSHIP WITHOUT COMPROMISE

There are many bridges that must be built in the life of the leader. There is not time or space to list all the different organizations or groups that could work together in the kingdom of God. What is essential to realize is that leaders must partner together to reach the world for Jesus Christ. Campus Crusade for Christ has been privileged to work with tens of thousands of different churches, denominations, and organizations over the past fifty years. It has been amazing to find so many brothers and sisters in Christ in so many different contexts. We all serve the same God, and we all need each other to fulfill His plan without compromising our biblical commitments.

However, we cannot forget Paul's models in the New Testament. There are Demases out there who can cause us trouble and heartache. There may even be some relationships that, like Barnabas and Paul's, will start off well but will have the potential to end in disappointment. How can we protect our churches from these hardships and at the same time follow Christ's command to take the gospel to the whole world? Is it possible to avoid the problems? Probably not, but the few trials along the way are worth the glory of working in synergy. Jesus asked Peter to be His disciple, knowing he would deny Him.

Many are afraid of sharing ministry with those who have doctrinal differences. Some of these differences are major tenets of faith. While we do not suggest that individuals abandon what they believe, there are always areas of commonality in which we can work together. Through the years, I (James) have spoken in hundreds of churches to thousands of people. These groups have represented many different denominations and beliefs. Despite the differences, there were always areas where we could agree. These areas of agreement became the center of our working together.

> **It is important that each individual's distinctives stay in place as they collaborate.**

For over fifty years, I (Bill) have worked with anyone and everyone who loves our Lord whether these individuals were mainline Protestant, Orthodox, Catholic, or Charismatic. Together we have helped present the gospel to billions of people in the last few years. We could not have done this if God had not brought us together to serve Him together.

St. Augustine coined this axiom as a basis for agreement between believers of different Christian communities whenever questions of doctrine arise: "In essentials, unity; in nonessentials, liberty; in all things, charity." This is an excellent criteria to use when judging the legitimacy of a call to church unity.

In cooperating with other believers, it is important to follow seven steps to make the partnership the most effective. Leaders who rush into partnerships with others without planning often end up doing more harm than good. It is necessary to *grow* together before groups can work together. Each of us brings a truckload of baggage when we partner together. It will be necessary to walk through the initial stages of union carefully so that expectations are understood and no feelings are hurt. The one component to synergistic relationships that most ignore is time. It will take many hours of working together to create the trust and goodwill necessary to create strong relationships.

1. Know yourself. The first step before any partnership can be formed is for leaders to know who they are and what they are called to do (as discussed in Chapter 4). If leaders are confused about their mission, their mission will be lost when they combine forces with those who have a clear mission. It is important that each individual's distinctives stay in place as they collaborate. In working together, they should not compromise who they are. Value each other's differences, as they are inevitable in life. It is the mosaic of faith that allows the message of God to be communicated to many different kinds of people. The goal of teamwork is not homogenization; it is cooperative fellowship.

2. Initiate cooperation. Someone has to start a relationship. Just like Barnabas, we must show initiative in starting partnerships. Working together does not start in a vacuum or overnight. It will take hard work and perseverance, so leaders must step forward with their hand out to join with others in leadership roles.

Many people talk about reconciliation and teamwork, but very few actually join a team. Great leaders move past talk into action. Seek out groups in your community that may need your help and groups that may benefit your ministry. Join ministerial alliances and prayer gatherings. Sponsor racial healing services with different ethnic groups. Allow your church to contribute its time and resources to the work of the kingdom in cross-denominational events. Remember the laws of God: "Whatever a man sows, this he will also reap" (Galatians 6:7), and "Give, and it will be given to you" (Luke 6:38). What you choose to invest in as an individual and as a church determines what will take place in you.

When we model synergy in our churches, we show the world that we value each other. We must not only talk about cooperation and interdependence, but we must also start the process of building it. There are many different components to the Body of Christ. Do not neglect Jesus' prayer that we would all be one in Him (John 17:21). Begin the necessary partnerships in your community in order that we might better reach the world for Jesus Christ.

3. Listen to and understand others. The greatest tool of any leader is the ability to listen. Marriage counselors have pinpointed the number one cause of divorce as a lack of communication. Communication means listening to and understanding each other. It is vitally important that we seek to understand the people with whom we want to cooperate. Most people do not listen with the intent to understand; they listen with the intent to reply.[4] When we work as teams, we must know where each party is coming from and what their expectations are. Many times, great churches and ministries have joined together to accomplish ministry goals but dissolved in failure. It is sad to see these united forces torn apart over misunderstandings and inadequate communication.

4. Share ideas; share power. In partnerships, authority must be shared. If one party has ultimate authority, there is no cooperation; there is a dictatorship. When the principles of synergy are in operation, each partner plays a vital role in the idea and power structure. Each member of the relationship should be able to contribute to the planning and execution of the ministry task. While resources and abilities will often require one member to be in the forefront, there will be times when other people's gifts will necessitate their involvement and leadership.

In sharing ideas, the group empowers each member to achieve the goals God has placed before them. Everyone has "ownership" of the ministry because everyone was active in creating it. In an information-rich society, those who know how to collaborate and share will be the leaders.[5] Effective cooperation requires humility and patience. Sometimes it will be necessary to place our personal agenda on the shelf for the greater good of the partnership. When we share with others, we must be willing to let others step into the spotlight as we step back.

5. Emphasize essentials. Campus Crusade for Christ and Cutting Edge International are para-church organizations. Our members and workers come from different church backgrounds and beliefs. Many people wonder how it is possible that so many people of different backgrounds can work together. The answer is simple. We emphasize essentials rather than majoring on minors. Let everyone else argue minutia while we work together to reach our world for the Lord Jesus Christ.

This does not mean we allow just anyone, regardless of his or her personal beliefs, to be a part of Campus Crusade or Cutting Edge International. We are committed to the essentials of faith. We believe in the lordship of Christ, man's need for a Savior, and the necessity of a life of holiness. These beliefs are found in our statements of faith. These statements of faith are our standard for working together in ministry. In areas in which we disagree, we follow the direction of Jesus and Paul: In all things, we must love each other. We can have the greatest knowledge in the world, the greatest methods of evangelism, and even miraculous signs and wonders; but if we do not have love, we are nothing (1 Corinthians 13). These truths are what allow us to work together despite differences in other areas of faith.

6. Be sensitive to others' needs. When we partner with others, the primary purpose cannot be our own gain. The self-centered, greedy, and self-consumed leader will become obvious to everyone. We have all been approached by an "overly helpful" individual who seemed to want to "be there for us." Usually these "helpers" turn out to be wolves in sheep's clothing. They want a relationship with us because they want something from us. We must learn to be givers, not takers. Being sensitive to our partner's needs is a vital part of teamwork. Take into consideration all aspects of partnerships, not just ministerial tasks. Evaluate the impact on the family, finances, and other relationships in which we are involved.

This is another expression of God's love in the world. When we work together, there will be situations that will arise where we can be a blessing to others. As leaders, we are gifted with talents and abilities that others will not have. When we are sensitive to our team's needs, those gifts and talents can be used for others, not just ourselves. They prepare us for the time when we will need help from others and their gifts come to the forefront. Be sensitive to the needs of others by helping them where they need it the most, not where we can benefit the most.

> The church is not only the sum of all its parts but also the relationship between the parts.

7. **Praise others and accept blame.** General George Marshall once said there was no limit to the amount of good people could accomplish as long as they did not care who received the credit.[6] Synergistic churches defer praise. Their leaders build others up; they do not promote their own success. No one enjoys working with someone who demands the spotlight. These people often do very little work and a whole lot of talking. It is these kinds of people who are not team players. When synergy is in place, we constantly try to find ways to lift other people up by acknowledging their contributions. This is not self-serving humility but true thankfulness for the people who make things possible. When we honor those around us, we increase their potential for doing more by increasing their self-respect, proactive living, and loyalty.[7] As members of a partnership, leaders should never gossip or put down team members but point out the positive things they have accomplished.

When mistakes are made, it is important to accept blame.

We cannot avoid taking responsibility when things go wrong. Those in leadership are ultimately responsible for the mistakes and setbacks that occur. Rather than pointing the finger at others, we should assume the responsibility for our mistakes. Those who work with us will appreciate our care and concern when we shoulder the load of responsibility. Nothing sours relationships like the blame game. In these partnerships, it ultimately does not matter whose fault it is but who will fix the problem. Dennis Waitley, a renowned author and much sought-after speaker, has often said, "You can always spot losers in life. The losers in life spend all their time making others look bad while making themselves look good. Instead of painting their house, they spend all their time throwing mud on their neighbors houses."

CONCLUSION

We must work together in synergy if we are to evangelize the world. Remember, synergy is when "the sum is greater than the parts." Fellow leaders must work in tandem with other churches of different denominations and ministry organizations to reach their communities. By working together, we increase our effectiveness, supply accountability for each other, and help each other through difficult times. These relationships are vital to church life. The church is not only the sum of all its parts but also the relationship between the parts.[8] The way we work together greatly affects the work we do in the world. Synergistic churches' greatest value is seen when they are a part of something greater than themselves.

The church must present a unified force to the world. It is sad that many in the world see the church as a bickering, infighting organization. We have allowed petty differences in church government and structure to fracture us into hundreds of pieces. Let us work together to reach our communities and create positive change in the world by helping to rebuild Christ's kingdom.

To do this will require trust and transparency, which are foundational to all relationships. Our character must never be in question. If the people you partner with cannot trust you, it will be impossible for you to work together. Part of honesty and trust is being open and transparent. The relationship must be built upon mutual cooperation and openness. Working together requires a level of knowledge about each other. If it is apparent that we are hiding something from the team, there will be less unity.

This kind of synergistic cooperation is seen in the new ministry launched from the Beyond All Limits Conference in Orlando, Florida, in January 2002. Various leaders from around the world gathered to focus the attention of the church world on working together for training. Together we can achieve more than we can ever achieve on our own. Southern Baptists, Methodists, Pentecostals, African-Americans, Hispanics, and a host of other groups and their leaders are joining together to form strategic partnerships for effective ministry. We are privileged to spearhead this new endeavor.

Leaders from various ministries and denominations have been meeting to determine what will be the most effective way to train harvesters for the harvest field. Through cutting-edge Internet technology and direct broadcast television, a new wave of opportunities presents itself to the synergistic church. We must capitalize on these new means of fulfilling the Great Commission and expanding the Church of our Lord Jesus Christ. To God be all the glory.

CHAPTER 8

Effective Communication

In 1960, President John F. Kennedy delivered this memorable challenge: "I believe that this nation should commit itself to achieving the goal, before this decade is out, of landing a man on the moon and returning him safely to earth." A computer scientist with the Apollo space program describes the impact this clear, focused, and demanding goal had on his colleagues:

> I have never seen a group of people work with such absolute focus and fervor as these people who saw it as their own personal mission to send astronauts to the moon. They worked incredibly long hours, under intense pressure, and they loved it. They had something that added meaning and value to their own lives, and they gave 200 percent to make it come true.[1]

Kennedy announced a vision that was in the heart of the American people. While many knew that America was behind the Soviets in the space race, Kennedy transformed that knowledge into motivated work by challenging America and the space program. John Glenn's giant leap for mankind was possible because of Kennedy's short statement years earlier. Kennedy was able to communicate the vision and desire for America to reach the moon. His declaration was more powerful than all the committee meetings, reports, programs, and even the process of reaching the moon. Kennedy motivated America by focusing its resources through communication of the goal.

PROCLAMATION AND THE CHURCH

Powerful churches are preaching churches. Most times, preaching does not fail because of logistics but because the preacher does not know his audience. People need to have their ears turned into eyes so they can see the truth. We must always remember that a person's mind is not a debating hall but a picture gallery. Leaders create great pictures in the minds and hearts of their followers. Through effective communication they enable the people around them to see what they could not previously see. Great churches are built upon solid biblical preaching.

As I (James) have crisscrossed America, I have discussed the subject of preaching at length and have perused hundreds of libraries belonging to pastors and churches. I have concluded that vibrant, evangelistic churches consistently hear Spirit-anointed, Bible-based preaching. The pulpit is no greater than the preacher who fills it on a weekly basis. Some pulpits have style without substance while others have substance without style. Today the need in preaching is for substance with style. The Christian and non-Christian alike are searching for truth in a generation filled with a valueless preoccupation with self and greed. Even though we believe that "everything rises and falls on leadership," we contend that every great church is led by a pastor who knows how to communicate the gospel effectively. The primary means of communication in the church is preaching; everything else is subsidiary to this.[2] Too much communication only presents facts to make people intelligent. Twenty-first century leaders must present the *truth* to set people free.

John the Baptist Came Preaching

John the Baptist was one of the greatest preachers of his day. Thousands of men and women in Palestine came to hear him proclaim the message God had given him. John the Baptist became the anticipated herald of the coming Christ, calling wayward Palestine to repentance. His ability to communicate and connect with people was matched only by the preaching of Jesus a few years later. Why did all of Israel, even their Roman masters, come to hear this eccentric prophet from the wilderness? What was it about John that was different? What made him a powerful preacher?

Looking at John's proclamation, he mastered three important components of communication: His message connected with the crowd, was centered on Christ, and called for a commitment. We must understand and master these three components if we are to communicate the gospel effectively.

Connecting with the Crowd

The man whom Jesus called the greatest man born of woman (Luke 7:28) captivated the thoughts of an entire region. His message was strong and convicting. His caustic words revealed sin in each listener's heart and brought conviction on all who came to hear him. Most of the people who heard him repented of their sins and were baptized. John the Baptist connected with the common men and women of Palestine unlike the Pharisees and chief priests of his time. This ability to connect and persuade the masses eventually became his downfall with the powerful religious elite. How did John the Baptist connect with the crowds that came?

1. **His message was** *practical.* Unlike the complicated laws of the Pharisees and Sadducees, John preached down-to-earth, realistic faith. He was not concerned with how many miles a person could walk on the Sabbath or how many times one should wash to become ceremonially clean; he was concerned with how people treated each other and the condition of their heart. John was questioned about how to live without sin (Luke 3:10–14). His response was not profound but practical, not complicated but clear, not extreme but easy. If you are a tax collector, do not extort money but do your job honestly and fairly. If you are a soldier, do not use your authority to take advantage of others but protect the helpless and defend the weak. Everyone should love each other and help those who are hungry or cold. John's practical message resonated with people who were burdened under the weight of religious jargon and seemingly impossible religious requirements.

2. **John the Baptist's message was also** *easy to understand.* He was more concerned about communication than oratory. His message was clear and concise: "Repent! The kingdom of God is at hand." There was no mistaking the content of John's preaching. Through metaphor and analogy, John created word pictures to illustrate the message God gave him that anyone could understand. He compared hypocritical Pharisees to snakes and vipers and talked of stones, barns, wheat, and fruit. John illustrated the power of God's cleansing with baptism and water.

We must learn how to connect with our audience as well. If there is no connection during our sermon, there will be no response to our invitation. When Jesus spoke with the woman at the well in Samaria, His point of connection was, "Give Me a drink" (John 4:7). He began with physical thirst before moving to spiritual thirst. What are our points of connection today? We can connect through stories of hardship and personal struggles, of family and friendships. By understanding the times, we can better connect with the audience.

Jesus demonstrated this principle. He engaged His listeners through common expressions and points of contact. He used stories, dialogue, questions, comparisons and contrasts, common experiences, metaphors, creativity, and imagination to connect the gospel to His generation. Just like John the Baptist, He was able to take complicated, abstract spiritual matters and turn them into simple concrete pictures that anyone could understand. The ability to make the difficult appear easy is the primary indicator of an effective preacher. We must enable every member of the church to understand God's Word and the vision God has given them to accomplish the Great Commission.

> If there is no connection during our sermon, there will be no response to our invitation.

Jesus often connected with His hearers by stories or parables (illustrations). "He did not speak to them without a parable" (Mark 4:34). A descriptive story helps people see the truth in everyday life. Thirty-three percent of all the recorded teachings of Christ were parables or stories.[3] Everyone loves a good story. They should be used to illustrate and clarify the truths of Scripture; however, sermonizers must be cautioned not to make the basis of their sermons contemporary stories. Stories move people, but the Word of God changes people. There must be a balance between meeting the needs of people and teaching the precepts of Scripture. On one hand, people determine the starting point of the sermon. On the other hand, the Scripture determines the subject and substance of the sermon. This is not abdicating the supremacy of Scripture or the biblical basis for the sermon, but simply underscores the simple truth that preachers must begin where the people are and not expect them to first come up to their level.

John connected with his audience, but he was also centered on Jesus Christ.

Centering on Christ

John proclaimed the coming of the Messiah. Though it was not until after Jesus' baptism that he identified Jesus as the Christ, he constantly pointed to the time when the Messiah would come. John did not fall into the temptation of promoting himself. He knew his calling was to prepare the way of the Lord. When others tried to lift him up and asked if he was the Messiah, John quickly pointed to the One who was higher than he, the One for whom he was preparing. He did not let his message become distracted by current issues or the popular topics of his day. John did not try to overthrow Roman oppression. He did not rail against the tax collectors. He simply called people to prepare themselves through repentance for the coming of Jesus Christ.

In humility and a servant-like manner, John proclaimed the coming of the Lord. When Jesus came to the Jordan River to be baptized, John knew he was not worthy to baptize the Messiah. Only after Christ's command did John agree to baptize Him. He knew he was standing before the Man whom he had been chosen to proclaim.

The apostle Paul declared to the Corinthians, "I determined to know nothing among you except Jesus Christ, and Him crucified" (1 Corinthians 2:2). Philip preached Jesus Christ to the Samaritans (Acts 8:5,12) and to the Ethiopian eunuch (Acts 8:35). The Seventy preached the kingdom of God in the name of Jesus (Luke 10:9,11). Peter proclaimed "peace through Jesus Christ" to Cornelius and his household (Acts 10:36). The central thrust of the fivefold ministry of Ephesians 4:11–16 is the maturing of the body of Jesus Christ. Jesus is not simply "an issue" in evangelistic preaching—He is the "main issue."

While many abandon the preaching of Jesus Christ today,

we cannot neglect the Savior of the world. Sadly, most preaching today reflects the self-help movement or financial seminars more than the message of Jesus Christ. We must never neglect the centrality of Jesus Christ in the messages we preach. Through our preaching, we must glorify and magnify Christ. Jesus Christ changes men's lives and brings salvation to the world. Preach Jesus Christ and Him crucified.

As a new Christian, I (Bill) was very impressed with a very godly pulpit orator, Dr. William Evans. Remembering my high school and college success on state and national debate teams and in oratory, I decided that I too wanted to be a great pulpit orator like Dr. Evans. Some time later, a godly pastor spoke to a group of us at seminary. He asked, "When you have preached your sermon, will people exclaim what a great preacher you are or what a great Savior you serve?" His question changed my perspective on preaching. Since that day, I have chosen to exalt and honor our Lord Jesus Christ in everything I speak or write. We should be known for the content of our message rather than the crafting of our message.

Calling for a Commitment

John's intent was not to share information and send people on their way; he called people to a commitment. Information that is not acted upon has no value. John knew he must call his hearers to interact with his message and commit it to their hearts. Rather than being a dispenser of facts, John led people to truth. The tax collectors would have to change their practices, Pharisees must quit their prideful acts, and everyone must repent of their sin before God. Without the commitment to change, the preaching of John the Baptist was worthless.

Teaching is not simply talking. Learning is not simply listening. What does it mean to communicate? The term "communication" comes from the Latin word *communis*, meaning "common." According to Howard Hendricks, commonness or commonality must first be established before effective communication can take place between people.[4] The more we build a commonality between the message and the listeners, the higher the level of communication between the audience and us. It is our responsibility to make sure the audience understands and applies the message to their lives. True biblical teaching does not take place unless the hearers of the message have learned and then acted on the new knowledge.

We will never see the fulfillment of our vision and goals if we cannot communicate them to others. We will lead only as long as we can communicate. As Christ's ambassadors to the world, we must model our preaching after John the Baptist's. Our preaching should connect with the crowd, be Christ-centered, and call men and women to repentance. It must be focused and powerful through preparation and the Spirit's anointing. The most powerful sermons are the ones that clarify, communicate, and stay consistently within the context of the author's intended communication.[5]

THE PINNACLE OF PREACHING

For most pastors and church leaders, preaching is the primary vehicle for expressing leadership and communication. It is the conduit through which Christ calls humanity to repentance and fellowship with God. Through the foolishness of preaching, God has chosen to save the world (1 Corinthians 1:21). It is the means by which the leader can cast vision and cause others to grow in Christ. Our communication helps foster and create the synergy that is necessary to carry out the plans and priorities of the church. It sets the tone for the effectiveness of the local church. Without solid communication, it will be difficult to nurture the synergistic spirit in the church.

In our attempt to communicate through preaching, it is important to understand completely the principles of effective communication. I (James) have identified an eight-step process for constructing an effective sermon based upon the principles of communication. We will highlight these eight steps here, but suggest you study them further in the books *The Preacher's Summit* and *The Pastor's Best Friend: The New Testament Evangelist.*[6] This preaching process can be applied to many different kinds of sermons (topical, textual, expository, etc.), but it was designed with the expository type in mind. Expository sermons put content, power, substance, and authority into our preaching.[7] Haddon Robinson defines expository preaching as:

> The communication of a biblical concept derived from and transmitted through a historical, grammatical, and literary study of a passage in its context, which the Holy Spirit first applies to the personality and experience of the preacher, then through him to his hearers.[8]

Each of the eight steps of the preaching process builds upon the others. They unite to create a powerful message that communicates Christ's gospel. They lead the preacher upward to the pinnacle of proclamation. Each step is intertwined with the others to create a message that is empowered and practically constructed so that the leader might adequately communicate the gospel.

Intercession

The first step in the process of proclamation is *intercession*. The leader or "proclaimer" is to be a praying person every day, not just when messages are being prepared for a church or crusade. Prayer should always precede preparation and preaching.

At every juncture in sermonic preparation, a "spirit of prayer" should be in the minister's heart. A preacher who is not praying in the ministry is playing in the ministry. One of the most important of all disciplines is to "pray without ceasing" (1 Thessalonians 5:17). He does not *stop to pray*; he simply does *not stop from prayer*.[9] It is interesting that Jesus commanded the disciples to go forth and preach the gospel, but he did not teach them how to preach. He did, however, take time to teach them how to pray. Many today emphasize the mechanics of preaching rather than the power of preaching—that is, prayer. Pray over and through all the steps of preparation and pray for the lost and the believers who will hear your sermon. Ask the Lord to direct every thought during your sermon preparation for the purposes of connecting, communicating, and converting the lost to Christ as well as strengthening the walk of the believer. Pray that God will enable you to communicate the vision He has given you.

The priority of the leader's prayer life will determine the power of his or her preaching. In studying the biographies of ministers God used in the past, you'll find that the common denominator is their priority on prayer. Mighty men and women of God have a consistent quiet time with God.

Illumination

The second step upward in the process of preaching is illumination. The unseen spiritual world is just as resourceful as the seen world of precise research and study of a Scripture—if not more so. In addition to practical exegesis, we must allow the Holy Spirit to illuminate God's Word to us. John MacArthur writes, "No clear understanding of Scripture leading to powerful preaching is possible without the Spirit's work of illumination. Powerful preaching occurs only when a Spirit-illumined man of God expounds clearly and compellingly God's Spirit-inspired revelation in Scripture to a Spirit-illumined congregation."[10]

There is a difference between inspiration and illumination.

Inspiration is the process by which men "inscripturated" the revelation of God. The apostle Paul needed inspiration in order to write the revelation of God (things previously unknown). While inspiration was the needed vehicle to reveal eternal truth from God to us in the Bible, illumination is needed today to fully ascertain the correct interpretation and application of a particular passage of Scripture. The anointing or illumination of the Holy Spirit teaches the meaning of the Word of God (1 John 2:20,27). The Word of God comes alive for the minister when illumination becomes a part of the preparation of effective evangelistic sermons.

While some preachers tend to ignore the role of the Holy Spirit in ministry or go to extremes in manipulating people, we must understand the balanced role of the Holy Spirit in preaching. The Holy Spirit is a gift, not a toy. There needs to be biblical balance both in the private area of preparation and in the public area of proclamation. Only the Holy Spirit can inspire a message and transform a carefully prepared manuscript into a message.

Interpretation

The third step upward to the pulpit of proclamation is *interpretation*. In order for exegesis to produce a thorough biblical theology, the minister must have a high view of scriptural authority. Scripture must have the final authority in all aspects of evangelistic ministry. Author David Larsen put it well: "If there is no difference between the Bible and Aesop's fables or Joseph Smith's tablets, we are abandoned with a hopeless mixture of truth and error calculated to foster hesitation and equivocation in the pulpit."[11] Our view of the Bible will determine how we preach it in the pulpit.

The meaning of the passage is achievable when the minister researches all the data. Evangelists and pastors must keep in mind that we are not called to *make* the preaching text relevant but to *show* its relevance. If Scripture is not already relevant, then the most gifted preacher cannot make it so. How does an evangelist or pastor make the Bible relevant to the churched and unchurched? How do ministers communicate a relevant message from Scripture to the present culture?

Historical-cultural research focuses the preacher back to the times and events of the original writer and will compel him or her forward to a current context. If modern leaders wish to transfer the relevant message of the past to the present, then the historical-cultural gap must be bridged. The historical-cultural gap is not crossed by allegorizing, spiritualizing, and moralizing the preaching text. Relevance is lost in a long, didactic discourse on the details of the preaching passage. People want to hear the message of the passage. Before we can make proper application of Scripture, we must know what the original writer through the inspiration of the Holy Spirit wanted to convey to his readers and must understand the unique challenges the modern hearer faces every day.

The total framework within which the biblical authors communicated and how that message relates to our own times is accomplished through grasping the whole before attempting to dissect the individual parts of a text. It is the total message that contains propositional truth. The sermonizer needs to look beneath the "surface structure" (grammar, semantics, and syntax) to the "deep structure" (the message behind the words). Answering why the text was written is at the heart of interpretation in order to apply the text to the present situation.

Last, the interpreter "principalizes" meaning into timeless truths.[12] The text sets the agenda for the sermon. Grammatical-syntactical exegesis (understanding what the text means by examining its word choice, sentence structure, and placement) and a historical-cultural background of the text (what events are taking place in the text that affect its meaning and presentation) reshape the preacher's understanding of the text. Expository preaching serves as the tool that evangelists and pastors should use to carry them from a biblical concept discovered through serious exegetical study to appropriate application for the congregation. A sermon constructed out of honest exegesis and sound hermeneutics will be true to the Bible in its purpose.[13]

Imagination

The fourth step to effective preaching is *imagination*. We live in a rapidly changing world. The attention span of most people continues to get shorter and shorter, and prolonged concentration of one idea is no longer effective. People are programmed to see and experience many different bits of information quickly. Too many speech instructors are teaching that speaking is a medium of words rather than a medium of sight and sound which happens to use words. People are asking, "Is your message worth the price I am paying?"

We need to remember that they do not see the world as other people see it but as they see it. Thomas Troeger wrote, "We assume that the world is the way we speak it, that reality matches the metaphors we live by."[14] Effective communicators understand how listeners imagine or view their world. The sacred responsibility of the preacher is to use biblically guided imagination to cross the bridge from the past to the present.

The imaginative mind sees how different facts and ideas can be mixed together to build a sermon. Just as a contractor knows how to pull together blueprints, brick, sand, and wood in order to build a house, the creative preacher knows how to tie together the parts of exegesis to form a "meaning" and the different aspects of homiletics to form a "message." The creative evangelist or pastor powerfully connects every word of the message to the next, forming sentences packed with pictures for the modern mind to understand eternal truth. Imagination arouses faith in

God and His Word. Imagination makes history come alive today. Imagination is one of the strongest allies of the sermonizer to change lives forever. It is often helpful to give "life" to a passage by retelling the story using our imagination and creativity, interjecting various cultural and historical realities into the story. This allows people to connect with characters in the story as well as with the message.

Imagination and creativity are to be used all throughout sermon preparation. Just like prayer keeps the proclaimer in tune with God, imagination and creativity will keep the minister relevant to the world. In order to be effective communicators of the gospel, preachers must stay in touch with the eternal world above them (God), the temporary world around them (nature and humanity), the pragmatic world within them (the body, mind, and spirit), and the life-changing world of the Bible.[15] The imaginative evangelist or pastor has the distinct ability to pull all of these worlds together into an effective preaching ministry.

> Illustrations awaken the five senses of a person and make the sermon easier to swallow.

Those who are the most creative have a structure to their presentation. Those who do not have a structure are slaves to chaos. We must be focused on our destination. How many times have we listened to a sermon and said at the end, "What was the main point?" "What did he really say?" When this happens, the speaker failed to create a powerful message.

Every message must be packaged in some creative way in order for the audience to grasp its meaning and be motivated by it. The biblical text determines the substance of the sermon. The sermonizer determines the structure of the sermon. Rick Warren states, "The crowd does not determine whether or not you speak the truth: The truth is not optional. But your audience does determine which truths you choose to speak about."[16]

Illustrations

The fifth step upward to the effective pulpit of proclamation is *illustrations*. Creative communicators are aware of the world around them and can find illustrations in many different walks of life. Just as the Holy Spirit illuminates the mind during the exegesis phase, illustrations paint pictures in the minds of the listeners during the preaching phase. Illustrations are not to be a substitute for solid scriptural substance; they are to illustrate various truths or principles throughout the evangelistic message. Illustrations allow the audience time to catch its breath mentally before diving down again for deep truth. Learn to use illustrations at the right time and place during a sermon to reach the maximum impact in the listener's heart. Stories stir the emotions, open the mind, paint pictures, help the memory, and keep the attention. Use a variety of illustrations in each sermon.

Timely illustrations can be found in books, magazines, newspapers, conversations, television programs, technology, the arts and sciences, sports, and most arenas of life. Look for them. Listen for them. Think about them. File them. Cultivate them. Practice them before preaching them. Illustrations are the "spices" that awaken the five senses of a person and make the sermon easier to swallow mentally, emotionally, psychologically, and spiritually.

The goal is to make the message relevant to as many people as possible every time you speak. We need to engage the whole person, or we will miss the opportunity to persuade them and motivate them at the conclusion of the message. The more involved the listeners, the more likely we are to convince them of our message.

Introduction

The sixth step upward to the pulpit of proclamation is the *introduction*. When does the introduction begin? The introduction begins before the sermon ever starts; people are "sizing up" the preacher before the sermon begins. They are judging sincerity, integrity, mannerisms, and believability. The experienced preacher knows the audience is watching during praise and worship, the special singing, and the offering. It is extremely important for the evangelist to set the tone of the message long before the actual sermon.

What are the qualities of a good introduction? Haddon Robinson has clearly described them as: 1) commands attention, 2) surfaces needs, and 3) introduces the body of the sermon. The introduction must be long enough to capture attention, focus on needs, and orient the audience to the subject, the idea, and the first point. Until this is done, the introduction is incomplete; after that, the introduction is too long.[17]

There are limitless ways to craft an introduction. The speaker can use an illustration, statistics, rhetorical questions, a paradoxical statement, a song, the Scripture passage, humor, authoritative quotations, or anything that grabs the hearers' attention. The speaker should view the introduction "not in terms of what begins your presentation but in terms of what will open up the audience."[18] This prepares the heart and mind to receive. The purpose of an introduction is to invite people into the arena of ideas with us.

Do not underestimate the impact of a powerful introduction. Remember, "the first ninety seconds of any presentation are crucial."[19] If the preacher does not capture the attention of the congregation at the very beginning of the sermon, the audience may never enter into the heart and soul of the sermon. It is imperative from the beginning and throughout the sermon that the preacher understands the audience's DNA: Demographics, Needs, and Attitudes.[20]

Begin to craft your introduction, illustrations, and applications by first discovering your audience's *demographics*. Whenever possible, make sure your content is relevant to the age group and socioeconomic structure of your audience. Know the general make-up and typical occupations of those to whom you are speaking.

We must also know the dominant *needs* of our target audience. What are their interests? What challenges do they face? The good communicator scratches where people itch. Be prepared to deliver relevant messages to people by knowing their needs.

Finally, understand the *attitudes* of your audience toward ideas and challenges. How do they feel about the subject? What motivates them? What is their perception of you as a preacher and as an authority? Do not change your message just because of their concerns, but be aware of their opinions.

Impartation

Personal power and charisma to persuade are not mysterious things that are only available to a privileged few. Some believe they cannot be earned or learned. This is not true. The effectiveness of our communication determines the effectiveness of our life. Leaders whom people respect and follow are those who are able to communicate effectively. They have a dynamic presence. If we desire to make a difference, we will have to learn to communicate with a powerful presence. We must be able to communicate what we desire to be accomplished in the church, in the ministry, and in life.

There is a certain amount of style in the packaging of a sermon. Jesus said, "I did not speak on My own initiative, but the Father Himself who sent Me has given Me commandment, what to say, and what to speak" (John 12:49). In other words, Jesus was led by the Father in all aspects of His speaking engagements. Attention must be given to the delivery of the sermon as well as its content.

What do we mean by the delivery of a sermon? It simply means to deliver "into the possession of the person for whom it was intended."[21] Lani Arredondo describes delivery as "the methods by which you communicate 'what' you have to say to the 'who.'"[22] Many people do not receive Christ because the sermon was not properly prepared and communicated with the nonbeliever in mind. It is possible for the preacher to speak the message, use up a portion of time, give an altar call, and still not accomplish the intended purpose of the sermon. It may be necessary to change the style of delivery for a particular sermon based upon the region of the world in which it is preached. Style may not be the major priority of preaching, but it is a major component of the preaching event.

The evangelistic message is delivered through the means of the verbal, vocal, and visual. Many ministers of the gospel spend most of their time thinking about what they are going to say to the audience, yet studies have concluded that the decision-making process of people is determined first by visual cues (55 percent), second by vocal (sounds and tones account for 38 percent), and third by verbal (actual words of the presentation account for only 7 percent).[23] This data reveals that the average person is persuaded more by feelings than by facts. The visual cues the speaker gives to the audience are positively or negatively persuasive. Mannerisms, gestures, head movements, facial expressions, platform movement, eye contact, and clothing project the overall presence of the presenter.

The vocal effectiveness of the presenter is determined by the quality and variation used during the preaching event. The voice should project the different "landscapes" of the sermon. There should be changes in volume, speed, and tone according to the content of the message. Pauses help the preacher and the audience to catch up with the message. Often these pauses are more powerful than words because they enable the listener to think through what was just said. Fillers should be avoided at all cost as they are distracting to the congregation. Stay on target with your message and do not become distracted.

The verbal persuasion of the sermonizer will be greatly determined by the choice of words and phrases. Emotive words drive home the theme of the message. The communicator must be enthusiastic about the message. Since only seven percent of the impact in the decision-making process is composed of actual words, every word and phrase of the speaker should be chosen carefully for maximum impact. We must always remember that we are not called merely to impress people but to influence their decision-making for Christ. We should know our audience at all times during the preaching of the sermon. This is crucial to effectiveness. A sermon is not too long because the clock says so; it is too long if the audience says so.

Invitation

The final step upward to the pulpit of proclamation is the *invitation*. The invitation phase is listed last because it is viewed as taking place at the end of the sermon. However, effective communicators begin their invitations in the interpretation phase, looking for bridges of persuasion. The end is viewed from the beginning. Life-changing invitations do not just happen at the close of evangelistic messages. There must be interpretation, application, and then invitation.

The invitation brings into focus the answer to the question: *What do I want to accomplish by delivering this message?* This is the objective actualized. When preachers have accomplished the objective, they can shout, "Bull's eye!" If thoughts, words, and actions do not support the objective or main thrust of the sermon, then do not include them. The invitation causes the audience to make a decision regarding the objective. By the conclusion of the message and invitation, people will _____. It is the presenter's responsibility to fill in the blank. As a result of hearing a sermon, people will be able to understand something or be able to do something.

193

What is an invitation? Allen Street defines it as follows:

> The invitation is that act by which the preacher of the gospel exhorts his hearers and instructs them how to appropriate the content of the *kerygma* in their individual lives. Any sermon that does not include an invitation as well as a proclamation is not New Testament–style preaching. Every sermon should aim to stir the human will. Truth is something that must be obeyed. It is the gospel invitation that presses home the claims of Christ and calls for an immediate response.[24]

Just as the first-century evangelist concluded the message with an invitation for people to repent of sin and place their faith in the Messiah for salvation, the twenty-first century evangelist/pastor should strive to invite people at the close of the sermon to receive the Lord Jesus Christ for eternal life.

The preacher must plan to issue an effective call for people to act upon the truth.

How does a minister prepare and give an effective public invitation? In order for an invitation to be persuasive, it must "be tied in closely with the major thrust of the sermon. In other words, it should grow out of the main theme of the message so that the people will not be surprised when it is given."[25] It should also be implicit throughout the sermon to prepare people for their response. The effective evangelist or pastor looks for ways to imply the invitation throughout the entire development of the evangelistic message. For some pastors, invitations flow naturally; for others, much practice is needed before the presentation of powerful invitations.

When the invitation is at hand, the preacher must plan to issue an effective call for people to act upon the truth. If we fail here, the rest of the presentation is useless. The key to a successful invitation is persuading people to place their faith in Christ.

Emotions can be aroused and the intellect stirred; but unless sinners are challenged to exercise the will and are given the opportunity to do so, it is unlikely they will do it on their own. This is why the public invitation is the hub of the evangelistic sermon. One of the greatest tragedies is the person leaving the service with the anticipation of accepting Christ but not being given the opportunity to do so or not being told how to receive Him into their lives.

CONCLUSION

After fasting and praying for forty days, Jesus announced, "The Spirit of the Lord is upon Me, because He anointed Me to preach the gospel" (Luke 4:18; Isaiah 61:1,2). Do you desire to be appointed by God and anointed by the Holy Spirit before and during your preaching ministry? When the preacher follows in the footsteps of Christ, he or she will experience the anointing of the Holy Spirit. When we preach, we are to proclaim God's Word with God's breath upon our words. We must inhale God's breath (His Word) during our study. Then we will be able to exhale God's breath when we preach His Word to a lost and dying generation. Ask yourself, "Did I take time to inhale today?"

Though some say the preaching event is no longer important, it is impossible to overstate the value of a solid pulpit ministry to the life and health of the local church. The leader and the church who are not communicating with the people who attend and the community around it are not taking their mission seriously. In fact, *Time* magazine profiled the importance of preaching in America in an issue on the most important influencers in America. It showed that the priority of preaching is surging in American churches. Duain Claiborne says that search committees for pastorates only want to know one thing: "Can the candidate preach?"[26] These churches have realized that dynamic programs are necessary for the local church in order to keep people involved; however, it takes dynamic preaching to attract them initially. It also takes dynamic preaching to keep them coming. Does preaching matter? Obviously. It matters so much that even secular news magazines recognize its importance. We fundamentally believe that great churches are built on great preaching.

CHAPTER 9

Heartfelt Compassion

The greatest fuel for creating synergy is love. Nothing else makes the mutual cooperation of individuals possible. Paul said we could have the greatest miracles and events happen in our lives and ministries; but without love, we are nothing (1 Corinthians 13:1–3). This love for others permeates all that we say and do. Our churches must demonstrate heartfelt compassion for people if we are to make an impact for God. The walls of our churches can only come down when they are pressured to fall by the power of love—a love for people.

This love for people comes from Jesus. Jesus Christ died on the cross for people. He came to seek and save the lost, not set up an earthly kingdom or a religious organization. Jesus was not interested in launching a movement or starting a denomination. He was not concerned with politics or the elite leadership. He was interested in people, all kinds of people. He did not try to stay with the wealthy and popular. We find Him with beggars and the sick, sitting by a well talking to a Samaritan woman, or looking up in a tree to find Zacchaeus, the tax collector. We find Him concerned about a rich young ruler and Jarius's daughter but still making time for children to sit upon His knee. Jesus spent time with lepers and prostitutes, showing them the compassion and love they had not felt in many years—if ever. He loved people, and so should we. As ministers of the gospel, our lives should be filled to overflowing with love for people.

As members of His Church, we must show the love and compassion Christ gave to the world. We must be active in helping restore people who are in need. One of the greatest avenues for showing this compassion in the local church is the emphasis on family. As society pulls down the family structure and sin wreaks havoc in the lives of men and women, we must rise up and protect the family, enabling it to become the center of love and compassion in communities. The love inside the church will never surpass the devotion of the home. Recently we interviewed Dr. James Dobson regarding the church and the family. He said, "The church and the family are the only two institutions left in America. If these two institutions crumble, western civilization, as we have known it, will fall apart." We must teach people the importance of loving their own families according to God's Word. We must also reach out to those in our communities who may be less fortunate and embrace them.

The church must be active in evangelism. Through love and compassion, we must reach out from the church and reach around the slumped shoulders of those who walk our streets. Moving beyond the limitations of insensitivity and apathy, we can show the love of Christ to those who are in need.

COMPASSION FOR THE FAMILY

Most church calendars contain a confusing mixture of events, prayer times, programs, and services. In most churches today, we have taken the command to assemble together very seriously.

In our desire to provide as many avenues of involvement as possible, we have often overloaded the church member's schedule. The greatest compassion the church can show is the protection of family time. We can do this not only by preaching and teaching on the family but also by scheduling and planning for time where the family can be together. One local church does not allow any activities to be scheduled on Monday nights. This is family night. This church values time with the family and protects it by not scheduling anything to conflict with it.

As Christian leaders, we must model this compassion in our own families. Too many families are morally bankrupt and emotionally drained because the minister's priorities are not correct. It almost sounds cliché to say, "We can win the world but lose our family in the process." Everyone is aware of the danger, but few do anything to prevent it from happening. We may think we are winning the world to Christ, but in reality, we have not won the world because we have not given proper attention to our families. Though Noah preached for 120 years that the flood was coming and no one listened, because of his righteous influence God allowed Noah's family to be included in the ark. It is in the ark of salvation that we are to shelter our families from the storms of life.

God has given us a responsibility to minister to and nurture our families. Anything, including church work, that harms or hinders this ministry is not from the Lord. It is a distraction to our primary, God-given responsibility. It has been said before, but leaders must have the following order of commitment and devotion in their lives:

- We must be committed to God first.
- We must be committed to our spouse second.
- We must be committed to our children third.
- We must be committed to our ministry fourth.

As synergistic leaders, we must have the private (God), the

personal (family), the professional (ministry), and the public (world) spheres in order. We cannot allow an imbalance in these areas. When these priorities are out of order, something will go wrong. Sadly, there are many sons and daughters of "powerful" ministers who will suffer eternal damnation because their fathers did not make time for them. God has called us into union and fellowship with our families before our ministries. God has given us a spouse to love and cherish, and our spouse's spiritual well-being is our primary ministry in this world. God has given us children that we might raise them to honor and love God. They are the primary mission field to which we are called to labor and disciple.

The minister's life is a complicated maze of responsibility. We are often pulled in hundreds of directions that seemingly make us choose between our family and other people. However, ministers must always strive to put family above the ministry. We must never let the work of God be the reason our spouse and children do not follow Christ. This will be difficult, but God will give us grace to accomplish His will and purpose in life as we give Him first place in our lives. When we live com-passionate lives that include our families, people will see and understand what we are doing. They will know why we are not able to be at every event and why we cannot always "be there" for them. We *are* being there for our families. When leaders put their family first, the community benefits; when leaders put the community first, both the family and the community suffer.[1]

The Ministry to Your Spouse

God said, "You shall love your neighbor as yourself" (Mark 12:31). The closest neighbor we have is our spouse. Most of us will be married as long as fifty or sixty years, as I (Bill) have been. My parents were married for over seventy years. If couples are going to spend that much time together, they should work at making marriage a lifelong romance. A relationship built on arguing and fighting is unrewarding and pointless. A marriage should be filled with love, laughter, prayer, worship, and service. It should be an adventure. Too many wives of church leaders hate their husbands and the ministry of the church. Their husbands are willing to help and serve anyone but their own children and spouse. Is it any wonder these precious, mistreated women turn their back on the calling of God? Pastors often unknowingly communicate to their spouses that they love others more than they love them.

> We must never let the work of God be the reason our spouse and children do not follow Christ.

We must be sensitive to the needs of our spouse and heed Paul's words: "Husbands, love your wives, just as Christ also loved the church and gave Himself up for her" (Ephesians 5:25). We are going to be together as long as we are alive; therefore, we should serve one another in love. Husbands are to love their wives sacrificially and steadfastly. Though we are responsible to love and care for our children, we should never allow our children to come between us. Our spouse is far more important to us than our children are. Children will be born, grow up, and leave home to start their own families centered on Christ. God has given our spouse to us for the length of our lives together. The most important person in each of our lives is our spouse. Just as Christ loved His Church, so we are to love our spouse.

Do not even allow problems to occur if possible. Plan ahead and guard the time together; do not allow situations to get out of hand. By doing this, we avoid having to constantly "make up" for mistakes. Many people think they can make up for missed dinners and forgotten appointments with gifts. Do not fall into the trap of substituting material love for time together. Because of the demands of ministry, many ministers will try to replace the time they lost with flowers and gifts. These are wonderful, but flowers wilt and fade; memories never do. All the gifts in the world cannot replace the joy our spouse feels when we cancel an appointment to take a walk in the park together. All the flowers in the world become insignificant when we turn down a speaking opportunity or cancel a counseling session to spend time alone with our mate.

God graciously gave Vonette a wonderful spirit as a wife and mother. We were married when I was 27 years old. By that point, I had built a self-sufficient lifestyle and had my own business. I knew the things I wanted and how to get them. I was active in church and chairman of the evangelism program. I was out day and night serving the Lord, dragging Vonette along with me, insensitive to her needs. I did not know any better, and she seemed to enjoy it as far I as knew. I look back and recognize how insensitive that was. There were no marriage seminars back then, so we learned to trust the Lord for His help as we went along. Now after more than fifty years together, we love God and each other more than ever.

Sheri and I (James) have traveled millions of miles in ministry together. From the jungles of the Far East to the inner city of Chicago, we have worked for Christ. Along the way, there have been many trials and testing times, disappointments, and even despair. However, the synergy we have as a couple is the sustaining power of our ministry. We all make mistakes; Vonette and Sheri can never be thanked enough for their sacrifices. There are not enough flowers in the world to make up for missed opportunities, but the couple committed to ministering to each other will be the couple that will make it through the hard times.

Does this mean everything is easy? Absolutely not! We all fail somewhere along the way. There are many times when we failed by not holding our wives' needs higher than the needs of the ministry. When this happens and we realize our mistake, we must take steps to rectify the situation. I (Bill) have done this in my life through a practice I call the "twelve words." These can be the most powerful words spoken when uttered sincerely and from a position of humility: "I was wrong. I am sorry. Please forgive me. I love you." These combined statements take us through a process of reconciliation. By saying "I was wrong," we *recognize* our mistakes. Saying "I am sorry" allows us to *reflect* on our mistake and show our sorrow. "Please forgive me" is the process of *repentance* before our spouse; and when we say "I love you," we *renew* our commitment to each other. Do not leave family issues unconfronted. Use the twelve-word formula or whatever is needed to be open and honest with each other and quickly admit mistakes. Sometimes the most important thing we can do is admitting we were wrong. We should not avoid mistakes or ignore them. We defuse potential problems by not allowing them to continue to develop and get bigger.

We should work on our marriage together by reading books by leading counselors and attending marriage retreats once a year. We must schedule special time away from other family members and friends to talk and develop our primary relationship in life. As we do this, we will fall more in love each day, and our ministry will be strengthened as we obey the commands of God.

The Ministry to Your Children

The greatest gift God gives people is the joy of parenting. God gives us a heritage in the children He brings into our life. Children can bring great joy or immense frustration into our lives. They make trips to the zoo and the park more exciting. The tears of a three-year-old can humble the greatest of kings, and the smile of a two-year-old can brighten the darkest moment. We invest ourselves in our children by spending time with them and participating in the important events in their life.

Our children are gifts from God that have been entrusted to us. We are to teach them about God and how to live a life of faith. They are the first mission field to which we are called. It is sad that so many ministers' children are far from the Lord. We must guard against this tragedy at all costs by pouring ourselves and God's Word into their lives from an early age. We should schedule our travel and meetings around their important events and performances. There is no substitute for being there.

When disciplining our children, we should not keep scolding and nagging them, making them angry and resentful. Parents often are too busy to give their children time to interact and talk. Listen to them. Do not be so busy serving God that there is no time to speak with them. This will cause them to become resentful, not only toward us but also toward God. Instead, bring them up with the loving discipline the Lord Himself approves. We must love our children and communicate with them, teaching them to love, trust, and obey the Lord our God above every other consideration in life (Ephesians 6:4).

Organizing the Church Around Family Needs

The church itself must have compassion on the family. Many times we ask so much of the members of our church that they do not have time to be together. According to George Barna, the average family in America is pressed for time together. Of the 168 hours available each week, adults spend 56 hours of that asleep. With the remaining 112 hours, the average American family devotes 50 hours a week to job-related events. This leaves only 62 hours a week for other activities. If the family attends church twice a week and is involved in a small group or some other activity, they can spend an average of 6 hours a week at church. This does not include any other extracurricular events or involvement in youth activities or groups. This leaves the family 56 hours a week to eat, attend to errands, and take care of any other matters in the home. The church must proclaim God's view of the family. We must create opportunities to guard this time for family learning and time together. The family should be the place where intimacy and fellowship take place. The family is where children should learn their ideas about God, relationships, philosophy, sexuality, and education. The family should be the most synergistic institution on earth.

To accomplish this, we must be careful not to make too many demands on people's time and energy. The members of our churches should not feel guilty for spending time at home together. We can help accomplish this objective through purposeful planning and teaching. Some churches have dropped a Sunday night service once a month and replaced it with a family night. Families meet at home together and worship in their own "small group." However, we must help people understand the importance of this special family time so they will give it the priority it deserves.

> The members of our churches should not feel guilty for spending time at home together.

Many churches have developed extensive, elaborate, age-based Christian education programs. These programs are testimonies to the creative power of a local church, but sometimes these incredible teaching machines can cause more harm than good because family members are constantly segregated from each other. In some churches, there is never a time for corporate worship. One churchgoer expressed dislike of this situation by saying, "I would love it if our church would put on things that I can do with my kids, not simultaneous to what my kids are doing. Sometimes I need a break, and I am grateful for things they offer which allow me to think and interact like an adult for a change; but more often, the problem for me is that I do not get to share these times with my kids because I am talking about kids with an adult class while my kid is off somewhere being a kid with the children of the other parents." Compassionate churches provide opportunities for families to worship together. In Joel's prophecy of an end-time revival, he calls for a time when all of Israel would join together for repentance (2:15–17). The old men and the young people, the babies and senior citizens were all to join together. When God's Spirit moves, it encompasses all of His people—young and old. We need to facilitate the learning of one generation from another.

We can create family times by scheduling healthy, uplifting, entertaining activities for the whole family. Synergistic churches can also create support groups and workshops to help singles, divorcees, abuse victims, and those with addictions. Pastors can preach a series on the family and have people sit together during these sessions. Many families feel stretched thin by commitments and responsibilities. The church must learn to accommodate family needs compassionately and teach them to value their families.

COMPASSION FOR THE LOST

Christ's love inside us compels us to love the world around us. While we can create loving families and communities inside the church, to be obedient to Christ's command, we must also love those outside the church. Pluralism and tolerance are sweeping the world. For the first time, Christianity in America is "competing" with many other faith systems. Islam and Hinduism are on the rise. New Age cults are attracting members every day. However, our compassion and love for people can separate us from these other groups.

Our world is reachable for Jesus Christ. If this is true, why has the Church failed to evangelize the whole world after two thousand years? The lack of world evangelization is not due to the size of the world, a growing population, false religions, political systems, or cultural barriers. When the Lord Jesus Christ was on earth, He did not plan to reach the world with the gospel single-handedly. The Master's plan was to equip His disciples for world evangelization. We have failed because we have not synergistically joined in a unified force of love to reach the world through personal and mass evangelism. We must passionately take the gospel into a dark world and train others to evangelize as well. The Church has not accomplished the Great Commission because we have failed to equip both the minister and the parishioner for evangelism and discipleship.

The walls of our church will be down as long as we allow the love of Christ to knock them down. For too long, the Church has endeavored to reach the world through addition and division rather than by multiplication. If a leader had the physical stamina to preach every night for 34 years to a crowd of fifty thousand people and at each meeting at least one thousand conversions were recorded, the leader would win more than one million people to Christ. He would have conducted the greatest revival in church history.

However, if that same minister reached and trained just one person for evangelism in one year and then that person and the minister each reached and trained one more person during the next year, there would be four people equipped as evangelizers after two years. If each of these four also reached and trained one person, there would be eight more trained at the end of three years. At first, this would seem to be a much slower process of world evangelization; however, after 34 years of each convert winning one person to Jesus annually, the total number of conversions would be more than 16 billion! If each person would win one person per year to Jesus Christ, the entire world would be touched by the gospel. We live in a reachable world.

Open-air and citywide crusades are effective tools for winning the lost. Local church campaigns are still vital in the overall life of the church. However, the greatest means of church growth and evangelistic revival is personal evangelism. Biblical revivals turn saints into soul winners. Spiritual awakenings cause cities and even entire nations to turn to God. In each of these events, leaders have led the way in cutting-edge evangelism, leaders who know how to surf the spiritual waves of revival for the purpose of evangelism and discipleship. Brian McLaren defines the mission of the church as "to make more Christians, and make better Christians."[4] This is the role of the truly missional community in the world. Will the rest of the world be told the good news of Jesus Christ? If not now, when? Will we make more, better Christians? If we as leaders will not lead the way, who will? We will never find a better time and better place to accomplish this global task. Therefore, let us arise together, ministering hand in hand in order that everyone might hear the gospel.

The Missional Church: An Army or a Social Club?

The synergistic church with its roof and walls removed turns into a "missional community." Mission means "sending," and it is the central biblical idea describing the purpose of God's action in human history.[5] The idea of missional churches in North America draws attention to the essential nature and vocation of the Church as God's called and sent people. Leslie Newbigin explains a missional church as a church that understands that God's mission calls and sends the Church of Jesus Christ to be a missionary church in its own society and in the culture it is in.[6] Missional churches are passionate about evangelism. They seek creative ways to influence the world around them with the message of Jesus Christ. Through love and compassion, they break through the barriers in men's hearts with the gospel. They understand their role in their community is to shine the light of the gospel. It is their job to reconcile the world to God through Christ's work on the cross of Calvary. They purposefully target people for evangelism.[7] They are passionate in their efforts to become missional communities reaching people for Jesus Christ.

Along with several other evangelistic leaders in the mid 1990s, I (James) was privileged to meet with Dr. D. James Kennedy to discuss worldwide evangelism strategies. During that time, Dr. Kennedy shared with us a powerful concept that has affected my understanding of evangelism ever since. He said, "Many people begin to complain when a local church begins to grow. They often say their church is too big, that there is no way they can ever know everyone." For Kennedy, if your goal were to know everyone, then you would probably prefer a social club. However, if we are trying to raise an army, then every church is too small. It will take a large army to touch and transform this world for the glory of God. What kind of church do you want? A church with walls is isolated and will always want to remain small. When we have a church with no walls, the limits are removed, and we are eager to grow. We need to view the size of our church not by the numbers who choose to worship with us but in light of the task of the Great Commission.

We are an army of passionate lovers—lovers of Jesus Christ and lovers of the world. We can expand as far as the love we have inside us will allow, and that love is unlimited: "The love of God has been poured out within our hearts through the Holy Spirit who was given to us" (Romans 5:5). Through love and compassion, we call men and women to a greater life that can be lived by walking daily with Jesus Christ.

Evangelism Beyond the Limits

As we journey into the new millennium, we now live in what some church strategists are calling a "post-Christian" or "post-modern" era. We can no longer assume that everyone has a basic understanding of faith and the gospel. Whereas much of the evangelism efforts of the last century were to turn nominal, Christianized people into full-fledged followers of Jesus Christ, evangelism now consists of turning professing atheists and biblically ignorant people into followers of Christ. Each group of people did not know God, but the manner in which we make the gospel known to them may be different because they begin at different levels of understanding. The love inside us compels us to help them come to Christ.

There are more unchurched people in North America than ever before. They do not understand the religious jargon (Christianese), practices, rituals, and in some cases, the purpose of the Christian faith. Elementary Christian concepts and beliefs once known by all are foreign to them. The individual at athletic events holding a sign that says "John 3:16" makes little impact. Few people even know what it stands for anymore, assuming the sign refers to "John" sitting in row 3, seat 16. Some may know the reference but are unable to understand the truth of the Scripture because they are alienated from the concept of a loving God. This lack of understanding has created hostility between the Church and the world.

Traditional methods of evangelism are not working. The gospel is in tension with a world that is unable to hear the message because of a dramatic difference in philosophical mindset and is unwilling to hear what we have to say because of false perceptions of who we are as Christians. We know that because followers of Jesus Christ are not accepted. They are even hated by the world because they are not of the world (John 15:18–23). Because of our love for others, however, we must reach past the world's stereotypes of unloving Christians and let the love of Jesus Christ flow through us as He reaches out to the unsaved person. Some churches' answer to this growing problem has been to become more aware of the needs and concerns of the unchurched. Their efforts are to make the church of Jesus Christ more easily accessible and understandable to those in the unchurched culture. The world around us must not be viewed as the bad outsiders with whom we fight, but as hurting neighbors who need love and grace. We must find creative ways to be a true missional community. We must find ways to make more and better Christians. We can do this because of Christ's love in us and it can be reflected through us.

COMPASSION FOR THOSE IN NEED

In response to God's love, we will want to share it with others. We must become channels of God's love to the world. John writes, "Beloved, if God so loved us, we also ought to love one another" (1 John 4:11). The world will know we are Christians by our love. We must be the hands of God extended in a world that has a false understanding of true love. As imitators of Christ, it is our responsibility to love a lost world to Christ. If we do not love others, our faith is bankrupt and John calls us a liar (1 John 4:20).

As sin wreaks havoc on the world, the plight of the less fortunate becomes worse and worse. Leading research agencies tell us that of the 6 billion people in the world, almost half live on less than $2 a day. Over 1.2 billion people live on less than $1 per day. In third-world and developing countries, almost 50 percent of the children are malnourished.[9] As followers of Jesus Christ, we have been called to minister to those in need—the hurting and less fortunate. We must have compassion for the hurting around us. True leaders are not arrogant or hateful, because the ultimate goal of leadership is to reflect the love of God in a loveless world.

The Importance of Compassion Ministry in the Twenty-First Century

Jesus said, "When you give to the needy, do not let your left hand know what your right hand is doing" (Matthew 6:3, NIV). Compassion ministry should never be seen just as a tactic of evangelism. It should not be trumpeted as our efforts for God. Jesus commanded that we love people and serve them for their sake, not our own. When we help people, our motives will show. If the people we help feel they are being tricked or used, any chance of ministering to them will be lost. We must love the people around us even if they never join our church. Ministering to them is a command of Christ, not a strategy of church growth. Many will see the love we share with God and want that same love in their lives, and this will make them want to come to Christ. While not all will seek to find Jesus Christ as their Savior, our loving them fulfills His command. We help those who are longing for love to find it in God.

The greatest testimony any church can have is that it gives back to the community it serves.

Compassion for the hurting is more than soup kitchens and Thanksgiving baskets. Our churches must become centers of love for everyone who needs it. Communities are filled with people who have deep wounds that no one is trying to heal. Synergistic churches connect with those around them by ministering to these needs. Churches like the Brooklyn Tabernacle have begun support groups and workshops for people struggling with addictions. Our society is filled with divorced people. Rather than ostracizing them, it is possible to minister to their specific hurts and help them through their crisis. It is the love we show to the lost that separates us from false religions and belief systems.

Large segments of our communities are shut off from hearing the gospel because of their circumstances. As the average age in America continues to climb, hospital and nursing home ministries will become increasingly important. Sending tapes of sermons and other church activities to shut-ins are key ways to bless those who are less fortunate. The physically handicapped such as the blind and deaf should not be neglected in our ministry outreach. Compassion for these groups of people is more than just having a place for them to worship with us. It involves identifying their needs and seeking practical ways to minister to them. A church without walls is not confined to a set location but goes wherever necessary to help someone connect with Christ. The greatest testimony any church can have is that it gives back to the community it serves. Churches should involve every member in compassionate outreach. For example, Pastor Tommy Barnett has integrated the theme "Find a Need and Meet It!" in the life of his church, Phoenix First Assembly of God. The faithful service of the members has led to phenomenal church growth.

World missions is essential to the growth of the church. The synergistic church not only connects with its own community but also sends its people and its dollars to connect with those around the world. We can be active in the rebuilding of struggling, war-torn nations through worldwide relief organizations like Samaritan's Purse, a ministry led by Franklin Graham; Convoy of Hope, led by Hal Donaldson; or Global Hope, a ministry of Campus Crusade for Christ. We must teach the Body of Christ that it can be connected with other members of the Body even when separated by great distances. Believers in earthquake-shaken India are intimately tied to believers in America. The apostle Paul said, "If one member suffers, all the members suffer with it" (1 Corinthians 12:26). Because we are compelled by love, we must rise to help those around the world who are hurting. Missionaries must be sent to those who have not heard the gospel, the hungry must be fed, and the naked must be clothed. The local church can be a most powerful force to achieve lasting change in the lives of members of third-world countries. They can do this because they are compassionate churches who serve in obedience to our compassionate Lord and Savior.

CHAPTER 10

Cutting-Edge Creativity

O ne of the greatest limitations we will face in establishing a thriving ministry and church is not an attack of
Satan or people who may come against us. Rather, it is
found inside our mind. The ability to think creatively and to
move beyond the limitations that stand in our way is the greatest catalyst to synergistic ministry. Leaders creatively break out
of the boxes around them and approach life through a system of
understanding and values that are foreign to others. Creativity
fuels synergy because it enables the different elements of the
church to find new ways to connect with each other. Synergistic
leaders see and operate differently than others around them
although the context and surroundings are the same. They have
a different paradigm.

Once the different elements of the church are connected, it
is imperative for the church to seek and implement creative
ways to reach the world with the gospel. One of the great challenges all church leaders face is how to minister the gospel in a

postmodern context without compromising essential biblical truths. The *ways* God communicates His love and will for our lives can assist us here. The fact is that words are the outward expression of inward thoughts. God communicates His inward thoughts to the world in two ways:

First, He communicates His thoughts to us through the written Word—the Bible. Scripture itself tells us that the Bible is "God-breathed" (1 Timothy 3:16). God communicated His inspired Word to us by means of His very own breath.

Second, He communicates His inward thoughts to us through His incarnate Son—Jesus Christ (Hebrews 1:1,2). The person and work of Jesus Christ is the principal way God speaks to us in these "last days."

To be successful at reaching a postmodern audience, the minister of today must follow the pattern of communication that God has set. Leaders must be empty vessels, a mere suit of clothes for Christ to fill, so God can speak His inward thoughts of love and forgiveness to the world lost in sin. We must allow God to speak His Word through us using His breath. This spiritual dynamic happens only as we are fully surrendered to Christ. As empty vessels full of Christ, leaders are free to cross the bridge to a new world through the use of creativity and imagination, without violating scriptural standards.

A great misconception among many pastors is their belief that reaching the world with the gospel requires worldly paradigms. In Judges 18, the Danites learned the folly of using the world's methods to accomplish a spiritual task. They took Micah's idols in their foolish belief that his idols would assist them in conquering the city of Laish. Unfortunately, the tribe of Dan, instead of achieving something great for God, managed to introduce idolatry into the other tribes of Israel by setting up the idols to commemorate their victory. It was this act that, many years later, led to God's judgment of the houses of both Israel and Judah.

Rather than depend on the world's tactics, which can only lead to idolatry, church leaders must develop and use a biblical worldview as the grid for all they do in ministry. A church "beyond all limits" requires leaders who are dead to self, full of Christ, and are thus free to use imaginative and creative ways to connect with a world in hyperchange.

In Chapter 4, we discussed Sir Edmund Hillary's ability to see Mount Everest conquered. He had the kind of vision a leader needs to scale large mountains. Hillary's vision would not have come true if he had not creatively approached the challenge of climbing Everest. Many had faced the same obstacles before him and had turned back, but his ingenuity and innovation allowed him to go farther than anyone had ever gone. After Hillary proved it could be done, others followed. His accomplishment changed their paradigm. Hillary did not possess any special strength or skills; in fact, before he set out to tackle Mount Everest, he was employed as a beekeeper in New Zealand. He simply combined hard work with creativity. Not only had the mountain been climbed in his heart, but it had also been climbed in his head.

One of the greatest rewards of creativity is knowing that others will follow you to new areas of advancement. Roger Bannister had been told it was impossible to run the four-minute mile. Hundreds had attempted it before him, and no one had succeeded. It was suggested that a human being was physiologically unable to run that fast for that long, but Roger Bannister did it. Interestingly, in the year after he broke the four-minute-mile barrier, 37 other runners did as well. The next year, over 300 runners ran the mile in under four minutes.[1] What some had said was impossible, Bannister accomplished, allowing others to accomplish it as well. We all have mountains and four-minute miles in front of us. The challenge of leadership is to conquer these challenges creatively by using a new paradigm. In doing this, we will inspire others to conquer their challenges as well.

What are the foundational principles to building a dynamic

ministry? Do others succeed because they are smarter, more gifted, or simply get the breaks in life? Is it because they do not have any problems to contend with and everything seems to fall into place? Is it that they pray more than others? Are they just lucky? Or have they been able, through creativity, to break the paradigm around them? Like the men who followed Hillary and Bannister, we will follow in their footsteps doing tomorrow what could not be done today. How many remote regions of the world remain unevangelized because someone thought it was impossible to get there? How many people in the great cities of the world have not heard the gospel message because someone assumed the task was too great?

CREATIVITY FLOWS FROM CHRIST

A great truth of Scripture is the fact that Christ is the omnipotent Creator of a hundred billion galaxies. Consequently, He is also the *source* of all creativity. Paul remarks, "He is the image of the invisible God, the firstborn of all creation. For by Him all things were created, both in the heavens and on earth, visible and invisible, whether thrones or dominions or rulers or authorities—all things have been created through Him and for Him" (Colossians 1:15,16). From His preexistent role as Creator of heaven and earth to His humble life as the carpenter of Galilee, creativity was the mark of the Son of God. Because Christ is the sovereign Creator of all, we would be foolish indeed to try to create anything in ministry without depending on Him. Jesus said of Himself, "I am the vine, you are the branches. A branch cannot bear fruit of itself except it abide in the vine, no more can you except you abide in me. Without me you can do nothing" (John 15:5).

Practically, how do we submit our creativity to Christ? By submitting every thought to Him. Paul writes that we are to take "every thought captive to the obedience of Christ" (2 Corinthians 10:5). Only then can we have confidence that our creativity in ministry reflects "whatever is true, whatever is honorable, whatever is right, whatever is pure, whatever is lovely, whatever is of good repute, if there is any excellence and if anything worthy of praise" (Philippians 4:8).

Once we have surrendered our creativity to Christ, the effect is to stimulate our brains. Biblically, the mind and the brain are not the same thing. The mind is ethical in nature while the brain is physical. When we submit our creativity to Christ, we are being renewed in our minds. Once the Holy Spirit controls our minds and consequently our creative processes, this unleashes the vast potential of our brains to accomplish more than we could possibly imagine. I (Bill) have always believed that most people use only a portion of their brains in their work. The reservoir of untapped resources that God has placed in each of our brains presents an amazing potential for creativity in ministry.

Creativity Begins in the Mind

Most scientists believe that the human brain is the most complicated object that science has ever tried to understand. The whole brain contains nearly ten billion nerve cells. Because of the intricate complexity of the brain's circuitry, the number of possible interconnections between the cells of the brain is many orders of magnitude greater than the number of atoms in the entire universe. This is amazing! The vast elaborate circuitry of the human brain gives it a subtlety and speed that even a hundred supercomputers working in sync could never hope to match. Researchers believe the human brain is capable of reviewing up to 10,000 separate factors at once, giving new meaning to the question, "What are you thinking about?"

Did you know that the average person has over 50,000 thoughts a day? For most people in a 16-hour day, that amounts to almost a thought a second. That means day in and day out, our minds are constantly whirring with impulses, notions, and urges of one sort or another in that intuitive process we call "thinking." We need to look closely at this statistic. How many thoughts of the average person are actually new thoughts each day? Naturally, we must have some repetition for memory's sake, but the essence of creativity is our ability to accommodate as many new thoughts as possible. The worst-case scenario would be having the same thought 50,000 times a day!

A great barrier to creativity is thinking today along the same lines as yesterday, the day before, five years before, and even a generation before. The noncreative mind mulls over the same ideas and beliefs, fears and worries every day. The very act of entertaining the same thoughts repeatedly limits our capacity for new and creative thoughts.

To break the paradigm that binds us, we must become creative. To become creative, we must first take control of our thoughts. We must leave behind old, worn-out thoughts and open our mind to new ideas, new opportunities, and a new vision. We must change the way we think about our lives, our ministries, our world, and ourselves. This is literally all we really need to do in order to completely revolutionize our lives and change the way we think. We must determine to create new avenues to express new thoughts.

Our Thoughts Influence Our Lives

One of the most important foundational principles to building an effective ministry is realizing that *our thoughts influence our lives.* Scripture says, "As a man thinketh in his heart, so he is" (Proverbs 23:7). This is a simple and challenging concept. The thoughts we choose to occupy our consciousness will influence what we become. Rather than copying someone else's ministry, we should allow someone else's ministry to become a springboard and sounding board for new, innovative ideas that catapult us forward into twenty-first century ministry. Our thoughts are the most powerful forces shaping our lives. In fact, our thoughts are among the most powerful forces in the universe. We are where we are and what we are because of the thoughts that have dominated our minds. As for the future, our destiny is being shaped by our thoughts right at this moment. Therefore, it is very important that we allow the "right" thoughts to preoccupy our thinking. We know the vast majority of ministers do not achieve their full God-ordained ministry potential. It is likely that the majority of ministers do not even question where their thoughts are taking them. This is why knowing that our thoughts influence our lives is such an important key to personal ministry effectiveness. We are to take "every thought captive to the obedience of Christ" (2 Corinthians 10:5).

We must change the way we think about our lives, our ministries, our world, and ourselves.

Many people feel that once they have created something new, there is no need to maintain the creative process. The creativity needed to found Cutting Edge International did not end with the ministry's inception. For over twenty years, Cutting Edge has tried to do what its name suggests: Be on the forefront of ministry effectiveness. When we (James) began our ministry, we began a creative process.

When we (Bill) started Campus Crusade for Christ, we were pioneering in uncharted "seas." Very few ministries were attempting to do what we felt God had called us to do; however, we allowed creativity to dominate our outreach. We were not bound to any "one way" to do the work of God. We had no idea at the beginning of our outreach on college campuses that we would eventually produce the *JESUS* film. And yet when we produced the *JESUS* film in obedience to God's leading, we saw an even greater harvest of souls.

Focusing Our Thoughts

Once we realize that our thoughts influence our lives, we also realize the importance of taking control of our thoughts. This critical breakthrough gives us the power to decide where our thoughts are going to take us. When Christ has full control of our minds, our thoughts will be centered on His goals. We begin a systematic program of thinking about the kind of person He most wants us to become and the life He most wants us to live. Within a short period, we begin to steer the life God has given us in the direction the Lord wants us to go.

The first step in taking control of our thoughts is doing a "mental download." For a period of seven days, write down everything you think about. As best you can, keep a running list of all the thoughts that cross your mind during the day. Make sure your list represents a good cross section of the things in your consciousness. Include all the hopes, worries, expectations, burdens, people, places, memories, or daydreams—whatever occupies your mind even for a fleeting moment. By the time you finish, it should amount to a whole laundry list of subjects and a good inventory of the thoughts that are influencing your life.

The next step is to go back and take a critical look at what you have written. Ask yourself, "Where are my thoughts taking me? Are my thoughts taking me where I believe God wants me to go? What do these thoughts tell me about myself?" Once you have studied your thoughts, it is time to get your thinking on track. Set aside your "mental download" list and begin a "mental upload." Make a new list of the kind of thoughts that will support where you believe God wants you to go with your life. Evaluate all the main quadrants of your life and ministry. Read biographies of people you greatly admire, focusing not on what they *do* in the ministry but on who they *are*. Once you have their good qualities in mind, begin putting them into practice. Then in a surprisingly short period, the Holy Spirit will weave these admirable qualities into the fabric of your character. You can learn from others and use these role models to accelerate your progress. Study key Bible verses that will help you advance in these areas of life.

We believe that creativity makes the difference between succeeding and failing, between growing and shrinking, between sleepwalking and living. Too many churches are following the same ministry patterns and paradigms of fifty years ago. This is not to devalue what has worked in the past. However, we must be willing to let go of old approaches that are no longer effective in the changing environment. We can creatively reach another generation of unbelievers by first creatively addressing the needs of the church.

How do you approach the ministry to which God has called you? To be effective leaders, we need to strive for creativity. While others continue to think of the same excuses to justify ineffectiveness, the thoughts of leaders are fresh and innovative. We have taken control of our thoughts, and now our thoughts will help us to become the people God intends us to be.

Recently, I (James) was privileged to minister at the Holy Convocation of Liberty University in Lynchburg, Virginia, to over 5,000 students and faculty. At the end of that chapel service, I stepped off the platform and was met by a student. The young man said to me, "Dr. Davis, thank you for sharing your heart today. I greatly appreciated your message, it really blessed me." He gave me a card and walked away. I thanked him and did not think much of it until later that morning when I read the 3" × 5" card he gave me. Written in bold letters were words that have convicted me ever since:

I am not afraid of succeeding in life,
I am afraid of succeeding at the *wrong things* in life.

The more I thought about these words, the more I realized that all of us will be successful in life. The question is whether we are succeeding at the right things in life. The question all leaders must ask themselves is whether they are successful at the right things or the wrong things.

You can be successful at being lazy. Some people succeed at failure. You can even be successful at sin. The world is filled with successful sinners, but none of these are the right things to do. The leaders of the synergistic church are not just successful in life; they are successful at the right things in life. They understand that it is not good enough just to get things done; they must get the right things done.

In traveling around the world, we have found that the greatest pastors are successful at doing the right things. Many times we have met pastors and church leaders who were forced to leave their places of ministry because they did not achieve the results people expected of them. Oftentimes during conversation, we have found they were confused. From their perspective, everything was going well and they even thought they had been successful. Sadly, these ministers were often succeeding at the wrong things in their ministry rather than the right things. They had focused on the wrong goals because they were looking through the wrong paradigm.

THE SYNERGISTIC PROCESS
IN THE LOCAL CHURCH

Thomas Edison, the inventor of the light bulb, invented over 1,300 different devices and machines to make life better for us. During the journey of discovery that led to the creation of the first light bulb, Edison tried over 2,000 different experiments before he achieved success. A young reporter asked him how it felt to fail so many times. With a smile, Edison replied, "Failure? I never failed once. I invented the light bulb. It just happened to be a 2,000-step process." Edison knew that there is a process to being successful. There must be a step-by-step journey to lead people through the process of change and excellence.

Leaders are not made overnight, and great churches are not grown in a day. Edison was not more creative than anyone else; he simply was not satisfied with failure and never gave up.

In today's world, anyone can make a product or provide a service. With the right amount of energy and hard work, we all can be productive. The real challenge is to produce a cutting-edge product or service that is in demand. Creative people find a "niche" for themselves or their product that satisfies a demand. Bill Gates created an operating system for computers that enabled everyone who owned a computer to work together. McDonald's created a cheap, fast meal that enabled people to eat quickly. They both approached the market creatively and made their products and services special. Many people may copy them, but they blazed the trail.

This does not mean that Microsoft and McDonald's were created overnight. It took years for them to become the organizations we see today. These were years of creatively incorporating their new thoughts into their processes. As we lead the church, we must understand our thinking process and the creation of the ministry God gives us. Ideas will never see the light of day if they are not integrated into the existing system through a natural process. New ideas are wonderful and innovation is needed; but if there is no process for change or implementation, the ideas will never take root. Many great ideas, new inventions, and valuable changes have been doomed to failure because of a flawed process.

Change is inevitable, but the way in which we direct that change determines our effectiveness as leaders. Great leaders help people change because they want to, not because they have to. They do this through the creative process of innovation.

I (James) have identified the five stages of this process. We believe that if you implement this process into your leadership style, you will see maximum results. Each stage is vital to the success of the organization. Each step is unique but intimately tied to the rest of the stages. They build one upon another. There is no standard amount of time that a leader will spend in each stage. In some organizations, it is important to spend a lot of time at certain stages. This is determined by the group and the leader. What is constant is the necessity to go through each stage. If the leader tries to introduce a new concept or a change in direction without going through all the stages, the desired change will take longer to occur. People will not understand why or how they are to operate in the new environment.

At each stage of the journey, it is important to understand the needs and the reason the stage exists. Although change is necessary, most people resist it because they feel comfortable with the status quo. It is important to remember that people usually resist what they do not understand because they feel threatened. There will be people in your ministry who will initially be unable to see the vision God has given you. In fact, there will be people who will never embrace the vision or the process until after it is finished. There is comfort in remaining in the same place, but routine develops into a rut if one is not careful.

As an evangelist, I have been privileged to travel over four million miles worldwide. I have been afforded the opportunity to preach the gospel in more than eight hundred churches in America alone. While traveling, I have made it a practice to listen, to learn, to watch, and to write about outstanding pastors and churches. The leaders who have been the most successful are those who have understood this process and used it to their advantage. Whether it was launching a building program, planting a church, creating a new ministry, or leading their staff, the process takes place whenever people move from one way of doing things to another.

Stage One: Purpose Determines Our Priorities

Any change or creative idea must have a definable purpose. There must be a sense of mission in the church before people will be motivated to participate in any ministry. Change for change's sake rarely accomplishes anything. Just as there must be direction before the departure of a plane, the church will never rise to its full potential without a clear, definable purpose. The established purpose of the church determines what the leaders see as their priorities. If I am in a church and their purpose is to evangelize the lost, most everything I see as a guest is centered on soul winning. They place a high priority on soul winning and outreach. If a church has a threefold purpose, the priorities of the church are multifaceted. The purpose of a church is reflected in what it views as important. When we try new ideas that are in conflict with our purpose, we waste time and energy chasing things that will not ultimately help us.

The leader's purpose is often reflected in a mission statement. The leaders should craft the statement through prayer and hard work. Most people assume they know their purpose, but many have never really thought it through. Without a clearly defined purpose, someone else's priorities will run the church.

Do you know what your purpose is in ministry? Can you quickly and succinctly state your reason for being, your specific purpose, and the vital components of your life and ministry? If you have not come to terms with your own purpose, take out a pen and paper and write what you think your purpose is in life. Spend some time over the next few days determining what is important to you in life and ministry. Let your purpose in life determine your personal and professional priorities.

Imagine with me that a close friend from out of town comes to visit you. This friend, who has never been to your home or your town, calls you and asks how to get to your house. What is the first thing you will ask? Where they are calling from, of course. You cannot give directions without first establishing where they are. There are many pastors and church leaders who want to "get on the road" to the next destination, but they never check to see from where they are starting. When you go somewhere, it is necessary to leave one location in order to get to another. If you do not know where you are beginning your journey, you will never be sure of your final destination.

Stage Two: Priorities Dictate Procedures

Once we have established what is most important to accomplish, we develop procedures to achieve those goals. We put plans and policies in place that make it possible to achieve the end we desire. Everything we do has a purpose. The manner in which we conduct our ministry reveals our priorities. For example, the ministry that does not see financial integrity as a priority will have sloppy procedures for spending and accounting for money. The church that sees the education of children as a priority will invest in strong Christian education and possibly a Christian school. Whatever the procedure, it must be developed in light of the organization's priorities.

There are many churches that have procedures in place that do not accomplish the achievement of their priorities or goals. In some cases, no one knows why the church operates as it does; it has always just done things that way. These churches are led by their procedures rather than by their priorities. How they do things is more important than what they do or why they do it. Procedure-driven churches care more about organization than about advancement. They have rules for every event, forms to be filled out in triplicate, and never run out of supplies. They rejoice in small victories, never realizing they are losing the war.

When they allow the busyness of the church to interfere with the business of the church, they mix up the process. Eventually people may begin to question why they do what they do. If they see that the procedure does not match their priorities, they will abandon the procedure—or worse, they will become loyal to the procedure rather than to the priorities of the church. This stifles creativity and hampers church growth.

In examining a church's procedures, it is easy to spot its priorities. Many churches talk about soul winning, the lost, and evangelism, but they seldom give opportunities for people to be saved or equip believers for evangelism. Many churches talk about discipleship and spiritual growth, but do not provide opportunities for their congregation to grow through teaching and learning. Many spiritual leaders talk about church growth and building a great church for God, but come in late for work and give their golf game a higher priority. Our life and ministry do not simply come together. We have to create a magnet that draws the issues or ideas together; we communicate what is important to us by how we live our lives and how our ministries operate.

In making our procedures match our priorities, a simple five-step method can be used. Each step fits together to form the acrostic *GOALS*.

G – Gather the facts. Before beginning a new enterprise, research the information. Find out what is important to the church staff, the board, and the laymen. Spend time and energy to understand what is important to the people to whom you minister. Discover the benefits and drawbacks of establishing this new procedure. Does it match the priorities of the church? Is it the right thing to do?

O – Organize a plan. Great ideas must be organized. There is nothing more frustrating than to leave a staff meeting with great ideas and new, exciting ventures and then see them shelved or forgotten because no one took the time to organize how they would be implemented. Create a time line of things to do in future meetings. Freedom to succeed is found in organization while slavery is found in chaos. Large projects and changes need to be broken down into small, manageable pieces. Establish due dates for tasks and assign responsibilities to individuals. By putting names and dates to tasks, you raise the level of accountability for progress and establish a way to measure advancement toward the final goal. A vision becomes a goal when you put a date to it. Dates provide a sense of chronological progress.

A – Act on it. After the research is done and the plan is organized, it is time to put the plan into action. The procedure will never become a reality unless it is purposefully put into place. Work slowly as you take this new idea or plan into the life of the ministry. Communicate to all involved what the purpose and expectations of the new procedure will be. Explain how it fits into the priorities of the church. Do not let it take anyone by surprise but let them know in advance how it will operate.

L – Look back and review. After the procedure has been put in place, study it to see how it is progressing. It has been said that life is lived forward and learned backward. In any new procedure for ministry, it is vitally important to plan review time. See how the process is going and how it can be improved. Ask a series of questions: Would I do it the same way again? Is there a more efficient way of doing it? Does it meet the need for which it was created? Have our priorities changed since it was created?

S – Set new goals. We cannot be content simply to bask in the glory of accomplishment. We must constantly be moving forward in planning and goal setting. Too many people rest on their laurels of success, never realizing how much farther they could go if they would set new goals. Accomplishment and success are only the foundations for future growth and dividend.

Stage Three: Procedures Develop People

The most important component of any organization, church, or ministry is people. They are the reason we do what we do. People are why Christ came to the earth to give His life. Leaders must keep people in mind throughout the entire process. People need to be led, not driven. We establish procedures that enable people to accomplish the work God has called them to do. If procedures do not serve the people, they do not need to be in place. Synergistic leaders know the difference between "using things" and "using people." People are not expendable commodities that exist for our personal achievement and advancement. Servant leaders understand that we exist for the benefit of the people. Leaders must find ways to make the policies and procedures of their ministry enable and assist people. They depend upon teamwork to accomplish the priorities of the organization. If the procedures do not serve the people, they should be abandoned and new ones created.

How do leaders make sure that people are being served and better equipped in ministry? Leaders must communicate with those they lead. By immersing themselves into the culture of their church, leaders find out what people need and what procedures are working.

The closest group of people to the leader in a local church is the church staff. It is the staff the leader must understand and help first of all. Through creativity and planning, the church staff should become a team that effectively carries out tasks and accomplishes the overall mission of the church. The pastor serves as the primary motivator and facilitator for success. Leaders should encourage the men and women of the church to fulfill their vital God-given roles in the local church. Church leaders cannot accomplish the Great Commission on their own; they must enlist and then equip all the members of the Body of Christ to do the will of the Father.

Stage Four: People Determine Our Programs

When it comes to pastoring a church, we must understand people, and those people must come before programs. It is important to note that programs flow out of the needs of people and the purpose and priorities of the church; the church's purpose does not flow out of programs. Many pastors are looking for the "right thing" to do in ministry while they are missing what God is calling them to be in their community. There is nothing wrong with programs; they are vital to the health and growth of the church. However, they must never rise above people. When programs are more important than people, the church's priorities are out of sync. When Jesus walked the earth, He built relationships with people rather than establishing a formalized religion. In the local church, the five-year-old in the Christmas musical is more important than the success of the musical itself.

Stage Five: Programs Deliver Our Product

Our product is a relevant, packaged gospel and mature Christians. This package may come in many forms. It may be written, spoken, or crafted into dramatic presentations. Our goal is to creatively package the gospel and deliver it through up-to-date programs in the church. Programs achieve the desired result when they create synergy with the people of the church. Leaders do not look for the finished product of their work without first going through each stage of the process. Dictators demand results without process, managers demand process with no results, but leaders get results by honoring the process.

CONCLUSION

The effectiveness of leaders is determined by their ability to stay on the cutting edge of creativity and by their ability to implement their new ideas into existing structures. The same is true of the church. Without both the creative approach and the synergistic process, we will never experience sustained growth.

CHAPTER 11

Jesus Christ: The Model of Synergistic Leadership

No one epitomizes synergistic leadership like Jesus Christ. The greatest leader who ever lived modeled the eight principles we have discussed and incorporated them into His life. Over 2,000 years ago, the Son of God walked this earth and changed humanity. The goal of the synergistic church is not simply incorporating eight characteristics into what your church is doing. The goal is to be conformed to the image of Jesus Christ, allowing Him to live His life through us. In essence, we must become like Christ; and as we do, we will find that these eight principles are evident in our lives. As we grow in our relationship with God and better understand His marvelous attributes, we develop a greater confidence in Him. We know we are called, we allow our character to be developed, and we demonstrate our commitment to Him. The roof is off in our relationship with Him. As a result, we are filled with compassion for those around us. We strive to cooperate with others to fulfill our mission. We effectively communicate the gospel, and we lead with Holy Spirit–inspired creativity. Christ operated in harmony with the Father in heaven and reached out to the world around Him. He has removed the barriers and walls in our lives and churches. As the Head of the Church, He lived with no roof and no walls and is our model for life and ministry.

CONFIDENCE IN GOD

Jesus, of course, had an intimate relationship with the Father. His knowledge of the all-powerful and all-loving Father allowed Jesus to put His full faith and trust in Him. He drew confidence knowing that God was in control. He lived His life in light of His understanding of God.

He relied on the power of the Holy Spirit throughout His ministry. The Holy Spirit inaugurated His ministry (Luke 3:21) and directed where He went (Luke 4:1). Jesus was not just baptized with the Spirit, but He was also filled with the Spirit (Luke 3:21; 4:1). It was the Spirit of God upon Him who enabled Him to preach the good news and proclaim the year of the Lord's favor (Luke 4:18,19). He was empowered to accomplish His mission on the earth.

Many people are more dependent on their own performance than on the power of the Holy Spirit. They equate activity and busyness with effective ministry. They are doing more and more and achieving less and less. Is it not amazing that technology has provided the Internet, email, faxes, television, radio, electricity, automobiles, PA systems, and many other means of communicating the gospel—but we have not yet reached our world for Jesus Christ? However, a small group of untrained and under-equipped disciples turned their world upside down, inside out, and right side up for Jesus Christ. Was this because they were empowered and guided by the Holy Spirit, while we are motivated by our own programs? The Book of Acts could be summed up as follows: The Savior went up, the Spirit came down, the saints went out, and the sinners came in.

CALLED BY GOD

Jesus knew the God whom He served and what His own purpose was. He knew He was to glory in the Father and do His will. Jesus said, "I have come down from heaven, not to do My own will, but the will of Him who sent Me" (John 6:38). When Christ faced Calvary, He prayed that God's will would be done, not His (Luke 22:42).

Jesus knew He was sent to earth "to seek and to save that which was lost" (Luke 19:10). He understood His calling and knew He was to finish the race He was called to run. He was confident in who He was. He did not feel it necessary to copy others. When the Pharisees hurled accusations against Him and His disciples, He did not conform to their expectations. When they compared Him to John the Baptist, Jesus and His disciples did not replicate another's ministry or habits (Matthew 9:14–18).

Jesus understood that He was to serve those He had come to save. He was comfortable in being a servant even when all of Jerusalem wanted to crown Him king. Jesus knew that the deeper the service, the higher the significance. The night before He was betrayed, Jesus washed the feet of His closest followers. He knew that He had to reach for the towel first and the throne second. He understood He had been called to be the suffering Savior before He was to be the reigning King.

CHARACTER DEVELOPED BY GOD

Jesus Christ is the greatest example of consistent character the world has ever seen. He was obedient even to the point of death, and His character did not falter even in the greatest challenge of

His life. Paul wrote:

> Have this attitude in yourselves which was also in Christ Jesus, who, although He existed in the form of God, did not regard equality with God a thing to be grasped, but emptied Himself, taking the form of a bond-servant, and being made in the likeness of men. And being found in appearance as a man, He humbled Himself by becoming obedient to the point of death, even death on a cross (Philippians 2:5–8).

Jesus, the only person to walk the earth who knew no sin, poured Himself out on our behalf (2 Corinthians 5:21). He humbled Himself to take upon Himself the nature of man so that He might save the world. He persevered even to the point of dying on the cross that we might have life. Throughout His life, He faced opportunities to forgo the Father's will. For forty days in the wilderness, Jesus resisted temptations so that His character could be developed (Luke 4). He modeled to His disciples and to us the importance of integrity and consistency. He went the second mile—He finished the race.

COMMITMENT TO GOD

In studying Scripture, we find no one as consistent in demonstrating commitment to God as Jesus. Prayer, worship, and evangelism were top priorities and expressions of His commitments to His Father. It was His practice to pray to the Father often (Luke 5:16). He modeled and taught His disciples to pray while He was with them. He would pray in the early morning and late at night (Matthew 14:23; Mark 1:35; Luke 22:41). The greatest expression of Christ's commitment is found in the Lord's Prayer (Matthew 6:8–13). In teaching His disciples how to pray, Jesus revealed what was important in His life. He began by talking about His Father. The Father knows what we need before we ask; therefore, we should praise His holy name (Matthew 6:8,9). Christ taught that we should pray for the Father's will (Matthew 6:10). He did not come with a personal agenda or list of needs; He came in humility. He prayed that God would give Him, not extravagant wealth or riches, but simply His daily bread—the amount sufficient to remain dependent upon God. Christ modeled prayer as something that was for every person every day.

Jesus Christ knew the awesome goal of His mission. He traveled all over Palestine, working to see His mission accomplished. He followed through even to the point of dying a humiliating, agonizing death on the cross. He also knew the necessity of training others to finish the task after He was gone. Thus, He spent more time with His disciples than He did with the multitudes. There was no "Plan B" for Jesus. He came and walked the earth, pouring Himself into His disciples. They were His only way for presenting the gospel to the world.

INTERDEPENDENT COOPERATION

Jesus also revealed the power of relationships. He knew that God's plan involved people reaching other people. From those who followed Him, He chose twelve to be His closest disciples. He modeled the principle of partnership. When the seventy and the twelve were sent out to minister, He sent them out two-by-two (Mark 6:7; Luke 10:1). He knew the power and accountability that resulted when leaders partner together for ministry. Yet, it was one of the twelve who ultimately betrayed Jesus. Judas was selected by Christ to be one of His closest servants. Although Jesus knew betrayal was coming, He did not avoid working with others. The danger of joining with Judas was overshadowed by the fruitfulness of joining with Peter, James, and John.

As a member of the Trinity, Jesus' entire existence and ministry were in harmony with the Father and the Holy Spirit. He is the ultimate example of the power of partnerships. This is seen in the relationship we each have with God. No one comes to the Father except through the Son, yet it is the Spirit who draws all men to the Son. It was the Father who sent the Son, and the Son who glorified the Father.

EFFECTIVE COMMUNICATION

Jesus Christ was the greatest communicator in history. He proclaimed the truth of God to individual seekers (Nicodemus) and to the multitudes (the Sermon on the Mount). His words were simple and powerful. They brought people to repentance and life transformation. As a master communicator, He was able to disarm critics, inspire the hopeless, and convince the skeptics. He was anointed by God to preach the good news to all of Israel. Those who heard Him marveled at His ability to teach and preach (John 7:15). His message of hope and truth still rings in the hearts of those who read His words. Jesus' life and teaching modeled effective communication.

Jesus was a master teacher—every miracle He performed had a message and every sign had significance. Jesus never taught by accident; He taught purposefully. He answered questions and provided solutions to problems. If you are *weary in mind*, Jesus says, "Come to Me, all who are weary and heavy-laden, and I will give you rest" (Matthew 11:28). If you need basic *worldly goods*, "Seek first His kingdom and His righteousness, and all these things will be added to you" (Matthew 6:33). If you are *worried about life*, Jesus says, "Take courage, it is I; do not be afraid" (Matthew 14:27). If you want to be a *witness to the lost*, Jesus says, "You will receive power when the Holy Spirit has come upon you; and you shall be My witnesses" (Acts 1:8). If you are *weak in body*, Jesus says, "My grace is sufficient for you, for my power is made perfect in weakness" (2 Corinthians 12:9).

When Jesus proclaimed His message, He engaged the minds

of the listeners that they might learn the truth and then engage the hearts of the listeners that they might put the truth into practice.

Jesus was the *logos* (John 1:1), the divine Word of God on earth. Words are the outward expression of the unseen thoughts of the mind. God's thoughts cannot be seen, but He revealed those thoughts through the life of Jesus. Jesus became the outward expression of the hidden thoughts of God. He took blind truths and thoughts and turned them into reality for His people.

HEARTFELT COMPASSION

Jesus was filled with compassion. It was love that motivated His very presence on the earth: "Christ loved us and gave himself up for us as a fragrant offering and sacrifice to God" (Ephesians 5:2, NIV). Jesus came to seek and save the lost. He died to draw people to Himself. Whether it was the woman at the well, the thief on the cross, Zacchaeus the tax collector, or Nicodemus the teacher, Jesus wanted to give *people* an abundant and eternal life. He preached the good news of the kingdom of God and brought hope and healing to the multitudes. The last words He spoke on the earth were to command His followers to go into the entire world and make disciples.

Jesus and His disciples approached Jerusalem in the final days before the crucifixion (Luke 19:41). Seeing the city in the distance, Jesus wept. He did not weep for Himself, but for Jerusalem because they did not recognize the time of the Lord's coming and would soon be destroyed (Luke 19:44). The passion He had for His people caused great joy when they came to know the truth and great sorrow when they rejected it. Jesus wept because they would not know Him. When was the last time we as leaders wept for the people in our community who do not know Christ? If we are passionate for souls as Jesus was, there will be rejoicing and there will be sorrow.

Jesus also cared for His friends and family. He kept in contact with loved ones such as Lazarus, Mary, and Martha. While on the cross dying for the sins of all mankind, His heart turned toward the care of His mother. He comforted her and asked John to take care of her after His death (John 19:26,27).

CUTTING EDGE CREATIVITY

Jesus operated with a paradigm. He saw past the religious structures and human traditions of His day and brought a life-changing message to as many as would listen. He was creative in His approach to reaching people because the higher the predictability, the lower the communication. He preached, wrote words in the sand, cursed trees, performed miracles, turned over tables, and quieted a storm. He told parables and taught principles. He rode into Jerusalem on a colt and ended up carrying a cross. Jesus painted pictures for the creative side of the mind and preached principles for the cognitive side of the mind. In other words, Jesus engaged the whole person when He approached ministry.

Jesus lived His life in light of the process. He thought through challenges and prepared Himself and the disciples for the moment when their task would be at hand. He allowed them to prepare mentally for what would occur before the events of Passion Week. Jesus did not rush into ministry without first processing all the stages. He lived with the end in mind. He knew from the beginning of His ministry that the end would be the cross. His entire ministry can be understood in light of His preparing the disciples for the time when He would leave them.

CONCLUSION

The father of young boy spent all day at work looking forward to watching a baseball game on television. After he came home, he settled into his recliner. He was just beginning to relax and enjoy his favorite team when his 10-year-old son came in. "Dad, can we go play catch?" the son asked. The father, intently watching the game, told him to wait a little while and they would go play. After a few minutes, the boy asked his father again, "Dad, please, can we go play catch?" The father, reluctant to leave the comfort of his chair, told the boy to wait. After several requests and several "wait a little whiles," the father decided he would distract his son. Seeing a magazine with a picture of the world on it, he tore off the back page and cut up the world into very small pieces. Many of the pieces looked just like the others. He poured the pieces on the floor and told his son that when he put the picture of the world back together, they would go play catch. Settling back into his easy chair, the father assumed it would take hours for his son to "put the world back together." After 10 minutes, the boy ran to his father with the completed puzzle. The bewildered father asked how he had done the impossible task so quickly. "That's easy," the son replied, "On the back of the picture of the world was a picture of a man. All I had to do was get the man put together and his world came together."

We must become more like Christ if we are ever to "put the world back together."

Ministry beyond all limits requires that we put the person together first before we try to help change the world. We must become more like Christ if we are ever to "put the world back together." We challenge you to dream big dreams and cast a vision that will last beyond your lifespan. It is far better to shoot for the stars and land on the moon than to shoot for the trees and hit the ground. How high are you aiming?

Jesus Christ was the greatest leader who ever walked the earth. In less than four years, He took twelve men of diverse backgrounds and abilities and turned them into world changers.

In less than four years, He established a group of followers who would advance the kingdom of God until it swept the entire world. Through the power of the Holy Spirit and the blessing of the Father, the Son of God supernaturally lived His life and led His followers. He was and is the greatest example of a leader.

Ask yourself where you will be in twenty years. What will be your legacy? What kind of leadership will you give to those you are called to shepherd? We pray that God gives you the keys to unlock the puzzle of the future as we journey together, leading others by the power of the Holy Spirit.

APPENDIX A

Recommended Reading

The following is a list of resources to assist you in moving beyond all the limitations you encounter in your life and ministry. We have divided the resources into the eight distinctives (Confidence, Calling, Character, etc.) to better help you focus on your needs in ministry. This list is only a sampling of the many resources available for building a synergistic church.

CONFIDENCE

Bright, Bill. *GOD: Discover His Character*. Orlando, FL: *NewLife* Publications, 1999.

Morgan, G. Campbell, and Charles Spurgeon. *Understanding the Holy Spirit*. Chattanooga, TN: AMG Publishers, 1995.

Niebuhr, H. Richard. *Christ and Culture*. San Francisco: HarperCollins, 1986.

Packer, J. I. *Knowing God*. Downers Grove, IL: InterVarsity Press, 1973.

Stott, John. *Evangelical Truth*. Downers Grove, IL: InterVarsity Press, 1999.

Trask, Thomas, and Wayde Goodall. *The Blessing*. Grand Rapids, MI: Zondervan, 1998.

CHARACTER

Anderson, Ray S. *The Soul of Ministry: Forming Leaders for God's People*. Louisville, KY: Westminster John Knox Press, 1997.

Malphurs, Aubrey. *Values-Driven Leadership: Discovering and Developing Your Core Values for Ministry*. Grand Rapids, MI: Baker Books, 1996.

Maxwell, John. *Developing the Leader Within You*. Nashville, TN: Thomas Nelson, 1993.

_____. *Failing Forward: Turn Mistakes Into Stepping Stones for Success*. Nashville: Thomas Nelson, 2000.

McIntosh, Gary, and Samuel Rima. *Overcoming the Dark Side of Leadership*. Grand Rapids, MI: Baker Books, 1997.

CALLING

Barna, George. *The Power of Vision*. Ventura, CA: Regal Books, 1992.

Buford, Bob. *Half Time: Changing Your Game Plan from Success to Significance*. Grand Rapids, MI: Zondervan, 1994.

Jones, Laurie Beth. *The Path: Creating Your Mission Statement for Word and for Life*. New York: Hyperion, 1996.

Novak, Michael. *Business as a Calling: Work and the Examined Life*. New York: The Free Press, 1996.

Stowell, Joseph. *Shepherding the Church*. Chicago: Moody Press, 1997.

COMMITMENT

Bright, Bill. *Living Supernaturally in Christ*. Orlando, FL: *NewLife* Publications, 2000.

Carson, D. A., gen. ed. *Telling the Truth: Evangelizing Postmoderns*. Grand Rapids: Zondervan, 2000.

Davis, James. *The Pastor's Best Friend: The New Testament Evangelist*. Springfield, MO: Gospel Publishing House, 1997.

Guder, Darrell L., ed. *Missional Church: A Vision for the Sending of the Church in North America*. Grand Rapids, MI: William B. Eerdmans Publishing Co.,1998.

Hybels, Bill, and Mark Mittelberg. *Becoming a Contagious Christian*. Grand Rapids, MI: Zondervan, 1994.

Towns, Elmer. *Fasting For Spiritual Breakthrough*. Ventura, CA: Regal Books, 1996.

Warren, Rick. *The Purpose-Driven Church*. Grand Rapids, MI: Zondervan, 1995.

Zschech, Darlene. *Extravagant Worship*. Castle Hill, Australia: Check Music, 2001.

COOPERATION

DePree, Max. *Leading Without Power: Finding Hope in Serving Community.* San Francisco: Jossey-Bass, 1997.

Gangel, Kenneth O. *Team Leadership in Christian Ministry: Using Multiple Gifts to Build a Unified Vision.* Chicago: Moody Press, 1997.

Heenan David, and Warren Bennis. *Co-Leaders: The Power of Great Partnerships.* New York: John Wiles & Sons, 1999.

Maxwell, John. *Be a People Person: Effective Leadership Through Effective Relationships.* Colorado Springs, CO: Victor Books, 1994.

Maxwell, John C. and Jim Dornan. *Becoming a Person of Influence: How to Positively Impact the Lives of Others.* Nashville, TN: Thomas Nelson, 1997.

COMMUNICATION

Arredondo, Lani. *How to Present Like a Pro: Getting People to See Things Your Way.* New York: McGraw-Hill, 1991.

Davis, James O. *The Preacher's Summit.* Springfield, MO: Cutting Edge Books, 2001.

Henderson, David W. *Culture Shift: Communicating God's Truth to Our Changing World.* Grand Rapids, MI: Baker Books, 1999.

Olford, Stephen. *Anointed Expository Preaching.* Nashville: Broadman and Holman, 1998.

Robinson, Haddon W. *Making a Difference in Preaching.* Grand Rapids, MI: Baker Book House, 1999.

Wiersbe, Warren. *Preaching and Teaching with Imagination.* Wheaton, IL: Victor Books, 1994.

COMPASSION

Barna, George. *The Future of the American Family.* Chicago, IL: Moody, 1993.

Bright, Bill. *Five Steps to Sharing Your Faith: Leader's Guide and Study Guide.* Orlando, FL: *NewLife* Publications, 1996.

Hopler, Thom and Marcia. *Reaching the World Next Door: How to Spread the Gospel in the Midst of Many Cultures.* Rev. ed. Downers Grove, IL: InterVarsity Press, 1993.

Shawchuck, Norman, and Roger Heuser. *Leading the Congregation: Caring for Yourself While Serving the People.* Nashville: Abingdon Press, 1993.

Sjögren, Steve. *Conspiracy of Kindness: A Refreshing New Approach to Sharing the Love of Jesus with Others.* Ann Arbor, MI: Vine Books, 1993.

CREATIVITY

Covey, Stephen. *Seven Habits of Highly Effective People.* New York: Fireside Books, 1989.

Easum, William. *Sacred Cow Makes Gourmet Burgers.* Nashville, TN: Abingdon Press, 1994.

McClaren, Brian. *The Church on the Other Side: Doing Ministry in the Post-Modern Matrix.* Grand Rapids, MI: Zondervan Publishing House, 2000.

Rainer, Thom S. *High Expectations: The Remarkable Secret for Keeping People in Your Church.* Nashville: Broadman and Holman Publishers, 1999.

Sweet, Leonard. *Aqua Church: Essential Leadership Arts for Piloting Your Church in Today's Fluid Culture.* Loveland, CO: Group Publishing, 1999.

Wilson, Len, and Leonard Sweet. *The Wired Church: Making Media Ministry.* Nashville: Abingdon Press, 1999.

APPENDIX B

The Global Pastor's Network

In the future, the ministries that are not networking will not be working. The synergistic church is a church that works together. Through a new initiative entitled the Global Pastor's Network, hundreds of leading ministries and churches have come together to create a resource based upon synergy and cooperation. The Network is a global presence that provides digital training in multiple venues and multiple languages for every minister, church, and ministry in the world. Making use of the latest in satellites, Internet technology, and wireless devices, this network will provide resources and training twenty-four hours a day, three hundred and sixty-five days a year.

The Global Pastor's Network will augment the existing theological education with practical cutting-edge training that is as dynamic as the world that needs Jesus Christ. Walt Wilson, author of the Internet Church, states that God will use the Internet, just as He used the transportation system of the Roman roads, to reach the world for Christ. It is imperative that we make use of this valuable resource for the propagation of the gospel and the development of ministry leaders.

Research indicates that most pastors today believe they are inadequate to prepare and preach the gospel two or three times per week. This is compounded by the fact that many pastors do not have the time or the financial resources to improve themselves for effective, up-to-date, twenty-first century evangelism in their culture.

This lack of resources requires ministers to become more creative in their preparation for ministry. As the trend continues, fewer people will travel to seminary for formal training and will seek more accessible, flexible forms of training. The church is forced to reevaluate its current methodology for equipping men and women to lead the church.

Through the online Global Pastor's Network, the flexibility and accessibility so many require will be available. Through live audio and video streaming as well as archived material, the minister can instantly access a wealth of teaching from the leading educators of the church. In a matter of minutes, a minister can access the teaching of John Maxwell on leadership, Stephen Olford on preaching, or Billy Graham on evangelism. From their own office, seminary professors and renowned church leaders will teach one-on-one or to hundreds at a time around the world providing theological and practical training on topics such as prayer/fasting, family/marriage issues, money/stewardship, leadership development, effective communication, and evangelism. By establishing key training points in the areas of the world that have not experienced the technological growth, the Global Pastor's Network will continue to expand internationally. We believe that God is calling us to provide training to anyone, anywhere, at anytime.

We challenge you to take a few moments to log onto www.GlobalPastorsNetwork.org and become a member of this up-to-date, state-of-the-art, ministers' learning center.

End Notes

CHAPTER 1

1. This figure is based upon statistics gleaned from www.google.com on October 23, 2001.
2. Barna Research Group, "More Americans Seeking Net Based Faith Experiences," May 21, 2001, www.barna.org.
3. Shiloh Place Ministries, http://shilohplace.org/crisisin.htm.
4. Hyrum Smith, *The Ten Natural Laws of Successful Time and Life Management* (New York: Warner Books, 1994), 48–50.
5. Barna Research Group, "Annual Study Reports America Is Stagnant," March 5, 2001, www.barna.org.

CHAPTER 2

1. *The Oxford English Dictionary* 2d ed., vol. XVII, J. A. Simpson and E.S.C. Weiner, eds. (Oxford: Clarendon Press, 1989), 480.
2. Stephen Covey, *Seven Habits of Highly Effective People* (New York: Simon and Schuster, 1989), 263.
3. Ibid.
4. John Maxwell, *Developing the Leader Within You* (Nashville, TN: Thomas Nelson Publishers, 1993), x.
5. George Gilder, *Telecosm: How Infinite Bandwidth Will Revolutionize Our World* (New York: The Free Press, 2000), 265.
6. Laurie Beth Jones, *The Path: Creating Your Mission Statement for Work and for Life* (New York: Hyperion, 1996), x.

CHAPTER 3

1. J. I. Packer, *Knowing God* (Downers Grove, IL: InterVarsity Press, 1973), 6.
2. Stephen Olford, *Manna in the Morning* (Memphis, TN: Olford Ministries, n.d.), 10.
3. Millard Erikson, *Christian Theology* (Grand Rapids, MI: Baker Book House, 1985), 846.
4. John Stott, *Evangelical Truth* (Downers Grove, IL: InterVarsity Press, 1999), 87.

5. Erikson, 862.
6. G. Campbell Morgan and Charles Spurgeon, *Understanding the Holy Spirit* (Chattanooga, TN: AMG Publishers, 1995), 136.
7. Lyle W. Dorsett, "Ministry Maverick," *Moody Magazine Online* (Chicago, IL: Moody Bible Institute, 2000), www.moodypress.org/MOODYMAG/maverick.htm.
8. Bill Bright, *Living Supernaturally in Christ* (Orlando, FL: *NewLife* Publications, 2000), 156.

CHAPTER 4

1. Bob Buford, *Half Time: Changing Your Game Plan from Success to Significance* (Grand Rapids, MI: Zondervan, 1994), 20.
2. Stephen Covey, *The Seven Habits of Highly Effective People* (New York: Simon and Schuster, 1989), 108.
3. Michael Novak, *Business as a Calling: Work and the Examined Life* (New York: The Free Press, 1996), 34.
4. Laurie Beth Jones, *The Path: Creating Your Mission Statement for Work and for Life* (New York: Hyperion, 1996), 44.
5. Novak, 35.
6. Jones, 49.
7. Buford, 23.
8. William Bridges, *Creating You & Co.: Learn to Think Like the CEO of Your Own Career* (Reading, MA: Addison Wesley Publishing, 1997), 38.
9. Ibid., 39.
10. Statistics supplied by www.everestnews.com as of June 1, 2001. This number is an estimate.
11. Jones, xviii.
12. Leonard Sweet, *Aqua Church* (Loveland, CO: Group Publishing, 1999), 130.
13. George Barna, *The Power of Vision* (Ventura, CA: Regal Books, 1992), 12.
14. Novak, 35.

CHAPTER 5

1. Gary McIntosh and Samuel Rima, *Overcoming the Dark Side of Leadership* (Grand Rapids, MI: Baker Books, 1997), 41.
2. The Pastor's Story File, May 1993.
3. Ibid.
4. Reiner Scnippers, "equipping," *New International Dictionary of New Testament Theology*, vol. 3, Colin Brown, ed. (Grand Rapids, MI: Eerdmans, 1986), 349.

5. J. Armitage Robinson, *Commentary on Ephesians* (Grand Rapids, MI: Kregel, 1979), 182.

6. Tubingen Michel, "oikos," *Theological Dictionary of the New Testament*, vol. 5, Kittel Gerhared, ed. (Grand Rapids, MI: Eerdmans, 1967), 119–59.

7. A. Skevington Wood, *Ephesians Volume 11, Expositor's Bible Commentary* (Grand Rapids, MI: Zondervan, 1981), 59.

8. Joseph Stowell, *Shepherding the Church* (Chicago, IL: Moody Press, 1997), 254.

9. Michael Richman, "Scientist George Washington Carver," *Investors Business Daily*, 14 May 2001, 4A.

10. Max DePree, *Leading Without Power* (San Francisco, CA: Jossey-Bass, 1997), 163.

11. John Maxwell, *The 21 Irrefutable Laws of Leadership* (Nashville, TN: Thomas Nelson, 1998), 134.

12. Ibid., p. 221.

CHAPTER 6

1. Brian Mansfield, "Singing the praises of strong sales," *USA Today*, 19 October 2001, sec. E, p. 2.

2. Darlene Zschech, *Extravagant Worship* (Castle Hill, Australia: Check Music, 2001), 6.

3. Ibid., 11.

4. Helen Lemmel, "Turn Your Eyes Upon Jesus," *Singspiration Music* (Nashville, TN: The Benson Group, 1922).

5. Leonard Ravenhill, *Why Revival Tarries* (Minneapolis, MN: Bethany House, 1979), 23.

6. Stephen Olford, *Manna in the Morning* (Memphis, TN: Olford Ministries, n.d.), 2.

7. Bill Bright, *The Coming Revival* (Orlando, FL: *NewLife* Publications, 1995), 92–93.

8. Elmer Towns, *Fasting for Spiritual Breakthrough* (Ventura, CA: Regal Books, 1996), 17–18.

9. Dutch Sheets, "Fasting With Your Church for Goals," *Fasting Can Change Your Life*, Jerry Falwell and Elmer Towns, eds. (Ventura, CA: Regal Books, 1998), 171–176.

10. Walter Elwell, *Evangelical Dictionary of Theology* (Grand Rapids, MI: Baker, 1984), 382–383.

11. C. E. Autry, *The Theology of Evangelism* (Grand Rapids, MI: Zondervan, 1954), 32.

12. David Barrett, "Dawn Report: State of Christianity 2001 #7" www.jesus.org.uk/dawn/2001/dawn07.html.

13. Patrick Johnstone, "The State of World Evangelization: How Are We Doing? Are We Making Progress?" http://www.missionfrontiers.com/newslinks/statewe.htm.

CHAPTER 7

1. Karl Taro Greenfeld, "Blind To Failure," *Time* Magazine, 18 June 2001, 52–63.
2. David Heenan and Warren Bennis, *Co-Leaders: The Power of Great Partnerships* (New York: John Wiley & Sons, 1999), 8.
3. Randy Jumper, "Reconciliation in the Twenty-First Century: Postmodern Bridge Building," sermon delivered 8 June 2001, Springfield, MO.
4. Stephen Covey, *The Seven Habits of Highly Effective People* (New York: Simon and Schuster, 1989), 239.
5. Leonard Sweet, *Aqua Church* (Loveland, CO: Group Publishing, 1999), 192.
6. Heenan and Bennis, 279.
7. Blaine Lee, *The Power Principle: Influence With Honor* (New York: Simon and Schuster, 1997), 111.
8. William Easum, *Sacred Cow Makes Gourmet Burgers* (Nashville, TN: Abingdon, 1994), 110.

CHAPTER 8

1. John D. Beckett, *Loving Monday: Succeeding in Business Without Selling Your Soul* (Downers Grove, IL: InterVarsity Press, 1998), 142.
2. D. Martyn Lloyd-Jones, *Preaching and Preachers* (Grand Rapids, MI: Zondervan, 1971), 26.
3. Ralph Lewis, *Learning to Preach Like Jesus* (Westchester: Crossway Books, 1989), 86.
4. Howard Hendricks, *Teaching to Change Lives* (Portland, OR: Multnomah, 1987), 98.
5. Joseph Stowell, *Shepherding the Church* (Chicago: Moody, 1994), 276.
6. These books can be purchased through Cutting Edge International, P.O. Box 5143, Springfield, MO 65801, http://evangelists.ag.org.
7. Stephen Olford, *Anointed Expository Preaching* (Nashville: Broadman and Holman, 1998), 309.
8. Haddon W. Robinson, *Biblical Preaching: The Development and Delivery of Expository Messages* (Grand Rapids, MI: Baker Book House, 1980), 20.
9. William Quayle, *The Pastor-Preacher* (New York: Easton and Mains, 1910), 261.
10. John MacArthur, *The MacArthur New Testament Commentary: Ephesians* (Chicago: Moody, 1986), 102–103.

11. David Larsen, *The Anatomy of Preaching* (Grand Rapids, MI: Baker Book House, 1989), 25.
12. See Walter Kaiser's excellent book on this process: *Towards an Exegetical Theology.*
13. Haddon W. Robinson, *Making a Difference in Preaching* (Grand Rapids, MI: Baker Book House, 1999), 76.
14. Thomas Troeger, *Imagining a Sermon* (Nashville: Abingdon Press, 1990), 120.
15. Warren Wiersbe, *Preaching and Teaching with Imagination* (Wheaton, IL: Victor Books, 1994), 297.
16. Rick Warren, *The Purpose-Driven Church* (Grand Rapids, MI: Zondervan, 1995), 228.
17. Robinson, 160–165.
18. Lani Arredondo, *How to Present Like a Pro: Getting People to See Things Your Way* (New York: McGraw-Hill, 1991), 36.
19. Ron Hoff, *I Can See You Naked* (Kansas City, MO: Andrews and McMeel, 1992), 30.
20. James O. Davis, "The Paradigm of Preaching," *The Preacher's Summit* (Springfield, MO: Cutting Edge Books, 2001), 35.
21. Charles Brown, *The Art of Preaching* (New York: Macmillan, 1922), 15.
22. Arredondo, 65.
23. Ibid., 70.
24. Allen Street, *The Effective Invitation* (Old Tappan, NJ: Revell, 1984), 37.
25. Lloyd Perry, *Biblical Preaching for Today's World* (Chicago: Moody, 1973), 113.
26. Nancy Gibbs, "How Much Does the Preaching Matter?" *Time*, 158:11, September 17, 2001, 55.

CHAPTER 9

1. John Maxwell, *The 21 Most Powerful Minutes in a Leader's Day* (Nashville, TN: Thomas Nelson Publishers, 2000), 29.
2. George Barna, *The Future of the American Family* (Chicago: Moody, 1993), 173.
3. Ibid., 185.
4. Brian McClaren, *The Church on the Other Side: Doing Ministry in the Postmodern Matrix* (Grand Rapids, MI: Zondervan, 1998), 27.
5. Darrel Guder, *Missional Church* (Grand Rapids: Eerdmans, 1998), 4.
6. Eddie Gibs, *ChurchNext: Quantum Changes in How We Do Ministry* (Downers Grove, IL: InterVarsity Press), 51.
7. Rick Warren, *The Purpose-Driven Church* (Grand Rapids, MI: Zondervan, 1995), 156–157.

8. Joseph Stowell, *Shepherding the Church* (Chicago: Moody Press, 1997), 45.

9. *World Development Review* cited in *Living Like Jesus*, Ken Horn and James Davis, eds. (Springfield, MO: Onward Books), 263.

CHAPTER 10

1. Harvey Mackay, *Swim with Sharks without Being Eaten Alive* (New York: Fawcett Columbine, 1988), 79–80.

William R. Bright
Founder, Chairman, and President Emeritus, Campus Crusade for Christ International

From a small beginning in 1951, the organization he began now has a presence in 196 countries in areas representing 99.6% of the world's population. Campus Crusade for Christ has more than 70 ministries and major projects, utilizing more than 25,000 full-time and 500,000 trained volunteer staff. Each ministry is designed to help fulfill the Great Commission, Christ's command to help carry the gospel of God's love and forgiveness in Christ to every person on earth.

Born in Coweta, Oklahoma, on October 19, 1921, Bright graduated with honors from Northeastern State University, and completed five years of graduate study at Princeton and Fuller Theological Seminaries. He holds five honorary doctorate degrees from prestigious institutions and has received numerous other recognitions, including the ECPA Gold Medallion Lifetime Achievement Award (2001), the Golden Angel Award as International Churchman of the Year (1982), and the $1.1 million Templeton Prize for Progress in Religion (1996), which he dedicated to promoting fasting and prayer throughout the world. He has received the first-ever Lifetime Achievement Award from his alma mater (2001).

Bright has authored more than 100 books, booklets, videos and audio tapes, as well as thousands of articles and pamphlets, some of which have been printed in most major languages and distributed by the millions. Among his books are: *Come Help Change the World, The Secret, The Holy Spirit, A Man Without Equal, A Life Without Equal, The Coming Revival, The Transforming Power of Fasting & Prayer, Red Sky in the Morning* (co-author), *GOD: Discover His Character, Living Supernaturally in Christ,* and the booklet *Have you Heard of the Four Spiritual Laws?* (which has an estimated 2.5 billion circulation). He has also been responsible for many individual initiatives in ministry, particularly in evangelism. For example, the *JESUS* film, which he conceived and financed through Campus Crusade, has, by latest estimates, been viewed by over 4.6 billion people in 236 nations and provinces.

Bright and his wife, Vonette, who assisted him in founding Campus Crusade for Christ, live in Orlando, Florida. Their two sons, Zac and Brad, and their wives, Terry and Katherine, are also in full-time Christian ministry.

Dr. James O. Davis
Founder and President, Cutting Edge International

Dr. James O. Davis is known on five continents for providing straight-forward biblical solutions to difficult, contemporary problems. His gifted insight and dynamic presentation on life-changing principles provide encouragement to people in need of guidance for change in the private or public aspects of their lives. Dr. Davis has traveled over 3.5 million miles to more than 60 countries where the Bible's answers are relatively unknown. While preaching overseas at tent meetings, open-air crusades, church revivals, conventions, and leadership conferences, he has led thousands of people to discover the value of Christ-centered living.

Dr. Davis is equally dedicated to a stateside ministry that places the Church at the cutting edge of a spiritual awakening. He is involved in church crusades, statewide outreaches, and college campuses across the United States and Canada. Davis has also been a featured guest speaker at international pastor's conferences, Dr. Bill Bright's Annual Fasting & Prayer Satellite Conference, Amsterdam 2000, Dr. Jerry Falwell's Student Convocation, Liberty University, and other denominational conferences.

As National Evangelists Representative for the Assemblies of God world headquarters in Springfield, Missouri, Dr. Davis develops and coordinates the annual National Evangelists' Leadership Conference. Under his leadership, participation in the conference has grown from less than 100 to over 4,000 nightly. He serves on the General Presbytery for the Assemblies of God, on the Two-Thirds World Missions Board, as an adjunct professor at the Assemblies of God Theological Seminary, as well as other national and international committees where he represents more than 1,500 evangelists.

Dr. Davis earned his Bachelor's degree in Bible at Central Bible College and two master's degrees at the Assemblies of God Theological Seminary. His Doctorate in Ministry was awarded by Trinity Evangelical Divinity School. As an author and editor, he has provided *The Pastor's Best Friend: The New Testament Evangelist*, *Living Like Jesus*, *The Preacher's Summit: Reaching Your Maximum Potential*, as well as articles for numerous publications.

Dr. Davis resides in Springfield, Missouri, with his wife, Sheri. Their two children, Jennifer and James, reside in heaven.